I0521822

"In this compelling work, Hamstra masterfully illustrates the transformative power of personal narrative, demonstrating how authentic storytelling becomes an essential tool for leaders and influencers at every level. Drawing profound insights from the life stories of Jesus's twelve disciples, the author reveals how strategic narrative sharing can catalyze meaningful change and inspire others to reach their full potential. This is an invaluable resource for anyone seeking to deepen their leadership impact through the art of purposeful storytelling.

—**John Katsion**, PhD, Professor, Southwest Missouri State University

"This book beautifully captures how everyday moments of listening and connection can reveal deeper meaning within personal experiences. By thoughtfully interpreting these moments, Dr. Hamstra offers insight and clarity that resonate beyond the individual, touching the lives of others. It is a testament to the power of communication to inspire, influence, and shape individuals and communities."

—**Todd Terry**, PhD, Department Chair, College of Business, Davenport University

"Hamstra creatively engages communication insights with stories from Jesus's earliest disciples to help us glimpse different leadership principles and practices in our own lives today. His attentive reflection points not only to leadership in response to crises but also, more importantly, to elements of leadership that are consistently oriented toward shalom."

—**Rev. Chris Schoon**, ThD, Leadership Coach and Ministry Consultant

"Using the unique life stories of the 12 men Christ called by name, this book provides a unique look at how critical moments of formation are transformed into stories that enable us to lead with authenticity and compassion. It vividly interweaves biblical, historic, contemporary approaches to storytelling to help leaders appreciate the way even the most painful, vulnerable, and even disappointing parts of our stories become the elements that create connection with others and encourage and inspire others for the glory of God."

—**Mary Jo Burchard**, PhD, Leadership Consultant, Concord Solutions

In Their Steps

In Their Steps

What Jesus and His Disciples Teach Us about Sharing
Our Leadership Life Stories in Transformational Ways

CHRIS HAMSTRA

Integratio Press

Pasco, Washington

IN THEIR STEPS: What Jesus and His Disciples Teach Us about Sharing Our Leadership Life Stories in Transformational Ways

Copyright © 2026 by Chris Hamstra. All rights reserved. Except for brief quotations in critical publications or reviews, no part of this book may be reproduced in any manner without prior written permission from the publisher. Write: Permissions, Integratio Press, administrator@theccsn.com

This is a publication of Axios, a Division of Integratio Press.

integratiopress.com

Integratio Press is an Imprint of the Christianity and Communication Studies Network:
11503 Easton Dr.
Pasco, WA 99301

www.theccsn.com

Cover design: Carol O'Callaghan
Interior design: Atritex Technologies
Cover Image: Depositphotos

PAPERBACK ISBN: 978-1-959685-39-5
EBOOK ISBN: 978-1-959685-40-1

Library of Congress Control Number: available from the publisher.

Scripture quotations are taken from the Holy Bible, New International Version®, NIV®. Copyright © 1973, 1978, 1984, 2011 by Biblica, Inc.® Used by permission of Zondervan. All rights reserved worldwide. www.zondervan.com. The "NIV" and "New International Version" are trademarks registered in the United States Patent and Trademark Office by Biblica, Inc.®

Dedication

To my children and grandchildren. May your stories
reflect Christ.

Table of Contents

TABLE OF CONTENTS

SECTION THREE: WITNESSES TO SHALOM

Acknowledgments

THIS BOOK IS DEVELOPED THROUGH LIFE experiences that span over 20 years. While I may miss a few names, please know that I value your insight.

The words that follow are meant to point you to a stronger relationship with Jesus Christ. The Lord's consistent presence in a chaotic world continues to provide for me the peace and confidence to take a small step each day. Thank you, Jesus, for the greatest story ever told.

My beautiful bride Dawnette is a huge encouragement. Thanks for your belief as this book took shape during Summer 2023. Thanks also to my children Mac, Micah, Noah, Mitch, Madison, Eric, Gabe, and Charlotte. Our prayer is that you grow in your leadership life stories through the overwhelming love of Jesus Christ.

There have been many reviews to fine tune the ideas in this book. Thanks to colleagues Vince Sharbo, John Katsion, Todd Terry, Greg Woodard, Chris Schoon, Russ Huizing, Mary Jo Burchard, Laura Lee Groves, and my mother Beth Hamstra. Thanks to Chad Allen and the folks at Book Camp for the resources and encouragement.

These pages have valuable insight from around the globe. The encouragement that stories and leadership can come together help me to continue the work. Thanks to Karl, Einar, and Audrey (Iceland), Harriet, Matthjis, and Claudia (Netherlands), and Dimitra (Greece).

Finally, thanks to Robert H. Woods Jr., Editor-in-Chief at Integratio Press. Your support and continued push for the best possible book are seen in the pages that follow.

Introduction

ONE OF MY FAVORITE BIBLE STORIES is depicted in William Brassey Hole's painting entitled "Jesus Walking upon the Sea." The artist shows Jesus walking on water toward the 12 disciples who are struggling to stay afloat in a small fishing boat. The waves churn on the Sea of Galilee and the clouds look angry and dark, with the full moon just starting to show through.

What catches my eye is the focus of the picture; in fact, this picture's focus changes my focus as I consider the story. Most sermons recounting this biblical event make Jesus and his actions the focal point. Hole's painting, however, focuses the scene on the boat and the 12 disciples. The artist places Jesus off to the right as a misty, ghost-like figure making his way across the waves. The bigger object, centered and dominating the frame, is the boat. When I look at this painting, my eyes and mind are drawn from the boat to the 12 individuals fighting for their lives.

This story is recorded in the gospels of Matthew, Mark, and Luke. After preaching all day, Jesus tells the disciples to get into the boat and go across the lake where he will meet them later. A storm swoops in and the disciples— some of them fishermen familiar with boats and water and weather—struggle to get to the other side. Waves swamp the boat and the winds scream across the sky. The boat, full of fearful disciples, is tossed about on the waves.

The painting depicts a chaotic scene. Several disciples are on the oars of the fishing boat, trying to muscle through the waves. Two are high in the mast, working to wrestle the torn sail around the crossbeam. Some are scared, curled up in the bottom of the boat, wishing the nightmare would end. As one of the disciples reaches out from the back of the boat, both arms high above his head, he appears to be pleading for the tiny ghost-like speck that is Jesus to hurry up and save them.

My imagination puts me right in the middle of the boat and the chaos. I can feel the gut-churning up and down of the waves and the boat being tossed left and right. I can feel the spray of the water on my face. I can see the waves crash over the side and pool around my feet. I can hear the wind as it howls across the sea and snaps the torn sails.

1

This picture, a visual representation of one story, not only piques my curiosity about the 12 different stories of the disciples in that boat but also about the One walking toward them. These men had different personalities, different perspectives, different temperaments, and different experiences. Yet Jesus intentionally walks through the wind, the rain, and the waves to connect with each of these individual stories. Jesus gets in the boat with the disciples and continues to work with each of them so that the individual stories become united in one Glory Story. By *Glory Story* I mean the perfect work of Jesus Christ shown in the Bible. God created a perfect world through creation. When sin separated humanity from Him, a sacrifice was needed. Jesus was born, lived a sinless life and was crucified on the cross. The story does not end there. Jesus conquered death and rose from the grave and lives today. The Glory Story is the free gift of salvation and eternal life to all who believe in Jesus. Just like the original 12, Jesus continues to do this today with us and with our leadership life stories. But what do I mean by leadership life stories?

Components of Leadership Life Stories

The idea of *leadership life stories* come from three articles by professor Boas Shamir. For over three decades, Shamir made a significant mark on leadership studies. While primarily known for his work in the area of charisma, he also wrote about leadership life stories. Shamir writes that "the life-story provides the authentic leader with a 'meaning system' from which to feel, think, and act."[1] This meaning-centered perspective of leadership is socially constructed within the process of human communication as leaders get to know themselves and create meaning with others.

Borrowing from this starting point, I define a leadership life story as a pivotal life experience (both formative and fortuitous) that provides a turning point in life. This leadership moment is reflected upon to construct a new meaning, which is then shared with others through a story. There are three important aspects of this definition.

1. **Pivotal Life Experiences**. These formative and fortuitous moments are remembered situations in life that connect to leadership. They can be positive or negative. They often leave a physical or emotional reminder. For example, a formative moment could be a promotion at work or a family situation in which you stepped up to lead. A fortuitous moment could be an unexpected quote that

stays with you or a situation in life that you were not expecting. It is important to remember that pivotal life experiences disrupt the planned life journey and provide a turning point in thought or action, specifically focused on leadership or leaders.[2]

2. **Reflection and New Meaning**. The ability to reflect on past experiences makes us human, differentiating us from all of the animals of creation. Each individual can make the intentional choice to pause, take a breath, and explore why these moments are important, leading to new meaning. We grow through times of reflection, making space for new meaning.

3. **Shared Through a Story**. This is the fun part of the leadership life story journey. Putting all the pieces together and engaging other people with stories can stir emotions and develop connection in ourselves and with others. Authentic connections that lead to transformational experiences are possible when we engage others, interact with the storytelling process, and create a sacred space.

When I look at Hole's painting, my mind is drawn in two different directions. I look back at the unique life stories of each disciple and consider how these stories point to the salvation offered freely to us in Jesus Christ. Then I look forward, wondering how lessons from these first-century leaders can be used in the twenty-first century.

Even in the confusion of the boat, I see the perfect shalom found as a disciple of Jesus Christ. The word shalom describes the moments throughout our day, in the middle of the chaos, that point back to the perfect goodness and harmony found in heaven. Quentin Schultze says that "shalom is an ancient Hebrew word that suggests the presence of God in our everyday relationships."[3] The story of the disciples struggling to stay afloat in the storm and the appearance of Jesus are an example of a leadership life story. I see a small taste of the perfect goodness of heaven.

We live in a world that daily seems to break us down and tear us away from the people and relationships that are important. Leadership life stories can bring people back together and share the goodness and grace of the perfect love of Jesus Christ. Lisa Sharon Harper in her book *The Very Good Gospel* breaks down the different aspects of shalom and concludes that "there is more than the brokenness, the destruction, and the despair that threaten to wash over us like the waters of the deep. There is a vision of a world where God cuts through the chaos, where God speaks and there is light."[4]

Old Testament scholar and author Walter Brueggemann separates the concept of shalom into two areas. The first sense of shalom is a cry for deliverance, an exodus and a search for the help and hope of the perfect goodness of heaven. In the painting, the disciple standing at the back of the boat with his arms held above his head might be shouting to Jesus for deliverance. As people of faith and leaders in a broken world we have these moments, as do our organizations, communities, and families.

The second component of shalom appears to be an opposite understanding. This sense of shalom is a solid faith and confidence, a resurrection that can see the good to come even though it is not here yet. As Brueggemann explains, "The focus is not an urgent petition for instruction into human affairs, but a settled, serene affirmation about the way the world is ordered."[5]

Leadership life stories are those moments for everyone in which they lead or are led by others and see a brief glimpse of the perfect goodness of heaven through their stories. Leadership life stories are those moments of crying out in the broken world and pointing toward the goodness and grace in the perfect harmony of heaven.

Just like the disciples in the boat, we too have experiences with chaos in our day that can point us to the perfect story found in heaven. Each of the disciples in the boat is a leader. In this story and in the turbulence of the storm, these leaders look up and see the perfect leadership of Jesus Christ walking toward them. From a perspective of shalom, Jesus in his perfect leadership shows us that our stories matter when we cry out for the perfect goodness found in heaven; he also shows us that our stories matter in those moments when we rest assured that God has everything in control, and we can take the next step forward in courage and with the confidence of Jesus Christ.

I invite you to join this journey of leadership life stories that can help build shalom in a broken world. The purpose of this book is to use the practice and process of storytelling to engage your personal leadership development. You will not only discover, develop, and deliver your leadership life story through examples from the 12 disciples, but you will get a glimpse of how their first-century lessons can be applied in building shalom today.

In Section Two, one characteristic of each disciple will be highlighted and connected to the practice of leadership life stories. Section One describes each disciple and highlights one or two characteristics. Our goal is to look at one specific characteristic of the disciple and, as the chapters develop, to create a holistic understanding of leadership life stories. The thoughts here are not meant to be an exhaustive examination of the disciples, but they will be fruitful. Looking back at each disciple's first-century leadership life story prompts us to look forward to twenty-first-century lessons for leadership today.

There are four brief but important caveats to consider as we begin this journey:

1. **This is not a formula**. There are no prescriptions or proven steps to follow that will suddenly clear up your purpose. This book is not a formula to follow step by step that guarantees peace and clarity if you follow it. This is a process that has twists and turns. The goal each day is to become more Christ-like in everything we do through the empowerment of the Holy Spirit.

2. **Leadership life stories demand your full engagement**. During this exploration, your whole body will be engaged. A leadership life story begins in your head as you rationally identify a formative experience. Your heart is then brought in to emotionally engage with the meaning. Your ears are then used to listen, your hands to write, and your voice to share your leadership life story with others.

3. **This experience will stretch you**. In the pages to come, we will identify moments of *what* and *why*. What happened in your leadership life story and how can you unpack its meaning? Why are these moments significant? Answering these questions may lead to times of difficult reflection and confession, but I can also guarantee times of great joy and fulfillment. The Lord uses both highs and lows in our individual lives to work out his plan.

4. **Leadership life stories require a community**. While some of this work takes place individually and in solitude, as disciples of Jesus Christ it is vital that we partner with others. I encourage you not only to plan times of solitude but also to surround yourself with community. Ideally, a significant other or family member can help you process the information. If this is not an option, consider friends around you who can help.

Organization of the Book

We will consider how our stories and lessons can help build shalom through a framework suggested by philosopher Cornelius Plantinga: Agents of Shalom, Models of Shalom, and Witnesses to Shalom.[6]

The chapters in Section One, Agents of Shalom (Chapters 1–5) demonstrate that all people have a leadership life story and all life stories matter. Leadership is all around us in the big and small moments of life. Often leadership comes to light in the big moments as a CEO makes a major decision or in the lives of great historical figures. Agents of Shalom also recognize the leadership that is seen and experienced in the small moments of life—for example, the simple conversations over dinner, listening well, or showing grace in hostile situations. While leadership is often defined in terms of influence certain individuals have over others, this book offers an additional meaning-making perspective which perceives leadership as service to others as well. Leaders and followers discover meaning together that points to a higher calling.

The chapters in Section Two, Models of Shalom (Chapters 6–9) develop four leadership life stories that can apply to our family, our work, and our communities. Some scholars contrast shalom as a movement from exodus to resurrection. In the middle of these two areas is the wilderness where much of the meaning is developed: "God acts in the moment of the turn. And the rest of our faith consists of reflection upon those moments in which our lives are changed."[7] As we examine these stories, we consider different situations we may encounter and how the basic techniques of telling a story can help us connect well with different audiences. These leadership life stories provide a small glimpse of the perfect shalom of heaven.

Finally, the chapters in Section Three, Witnesses to Shalom (Chapters 10–13) demonstrate how stories from great leaders of the past can help modern-day leaders serve authentically. As a witness to shalom, these leadership life stories provide examples of the tools we might use to lead ourselves and lead within different communities. These first-century leaders help twenty-first century leaders make a difference, aspiring to a greater good that reflects the Glory Story of Jesus Christ.

Let's return to the painting described earlier. While we have focused on the 12 disciples, it is important to remember that Jesus walks through the wind and churning sea toward the fishing boat. Not only does Jesus pursue the disciples, but he climbs into the boat and is intimately involved with each of the disciples and their stories. A personal relationship like the ones shared between Jesus and each disciple remains available to us today. Just as he encountered the 12 on the wave-tossed boat in the middle of the Sea of Galilee, Jesus intentionally engages us in the chaos of our lives. My hope is that through the stories of these disciples, you will begin cultivating your own leadership life story as you bring shalom, pointing this broken world to his Glory Story.

Discussion Questions

1. Reread the four caveats. Which one do you feel may offer you the greatest challenge and why?

2. As you consider the steps moving forward, what excites you the most? What are some of your concerns? Talk through some of these with friends and family as you begin this adventure.

3. Consider your life and your moments of leadership. Identify three places where you lead others and where others lead you.

Section One

AGENTS OF SHALOM

Chapter 1

Mapping the Journey

The Son is the image of the invisible God, the firstborn over all creation. For in him all things were created: things in heaven and on earth, visible and invisible, whether thrones or powers or rulers or authorities, all things have been created through him and for him.

—Colossians 1:15–16

I HAVE CARRIED A COMPASS for decades. A friend gave it to me as we hiked around the Garden of the Gods outside my hometown of Colorado Springs, Colorado. An old school forerunner of the modern GPS, a compass helps people get from one point to another.

A compass could be called a landmark of sorts because it provides direction on a journey; it orients you to where you are. As we begin this leadership life stories journey, it is important to figure out the landmarks we begin with and those we will encounter along the way. These can provide direction as we faithfully take steps forward each day.

Our first and perhaps most important landmark comes as we identify our point of departure. Where are you as you begin this journey? Your point of departure might be called a springboard or a jumping off point. A compass lines up with the earth's magnetic field, pointing north. Where do you line up? What do you point toward? Who or what serves as your compass?

Landmark One: The Glory Story and the
Cross as Points of Departure

This first landmark, the one that serves as the jumping off point for this book, is Jesus Christ and the cross. The overarching Glory Story of Jesus Christ is straightforward: Out of the overflow of his perfect love, God created humans in his image, distinct from the animals (Gen. 1:26–28). Adam and Eve sinned in the Garden of Eden and humans were separated from

God. To reconcile our sin to the perfect love of the Lord, a sacrifice was needed. Jesus was born, lived a sinless life on earth, and was crucified on the cross. Many end the story right there. In the Glory Story, however, Jesus defeats death, is raised from the dead, and lives today. Jesus served as our sacrifice so that we could taste eternal life through the free gift of salvation that is offered to everyone.

During his short three-year ministry on earth, Jesus chose 12 disciples. It is through these people that the church, which continues today, began. In his perfection, Jesus reached out and intentionally engaged 12 broken people who helped further the gospel and transform the world.

A focus on the Glory Story of Jesus Christ is our jumping off point as we consider our leadership life stories. Jesus Christ—"the image of the invisible God" (Col. 1:15)—is our spiritual compass; he is our true north. Oriented by him and his love for humanity, we look for three other landmarks as we seek to imitate Jesus and build shalom.

Landmark Two: Communication Involves Listening and Speaking

Communication is a form of interaction, and interaction begins with listening. Real human connection comes as we seek to understand and listen to others and then share our stories.

There are hundreds of definitions and models that attempt to figure out what works as people speak. This information is important, but the focus here is to think about why people communicate through the spoken word.

Faithful communication provides an opportunity to experience a small taste of heaven that suggests God's presence in every part of daily life. Communication professor and author Quentin Schultze writes that shalom comes from ancient Hebrew tradition. Faithful communicators can cultivate shalom, a foretaste of the joy to come as seen through the Trinity and the perfect unity of Father, Son, and Holy Spirit. We live in a world that is broken because of our sin. But even in our broken world, we can see, taste, touch, hear, and feel shalom, bringing it to those around us through our interaction with the Lord and interaction with others.[1]

I clearly see the Lord communicating through creation. Growing up in Colorado, I remember sunrises that peeked over the summits of 14,000-foot mountains. Later in life, God communicated to me on the beach, through sunsets over Lake Michigan. Some may experience shalom in the downtown sounds of a busy city. The Lord uses his creation as an opportunity to communicate with us each day.

Shalom can result from our interaction with others here on earth. We can see, taste, touch, hear, and feel the active presence of the Lord in our lives each moment of each day. Consider the sounds of a baby laughing or the excitement of a teenager. Shalom can be experienced without a word, through the gentle touch and a soft kiss between intimate partners. Old Testament scholar Walter Brueggemann cites a passage from the Book of Ezekiel as he writes that "shalom is the substance of the biblical vision of one community embracing all creation. It refers to all those resources and factors which make communal harmony joyous and effective."[2] Faithful communicators are surrounded by shalom.

Often these wonderful moments of shalom are missed, however, because we do not listen. The busyness of life can make listening difficult. This is a continual work in progress as we move through the stages of life with family and friends. Often the most profound lessons of life are learned in the quiet times. In her book, *The Story Factor*, Annette Simmons writes that "genuine listening has a deep, transformative power."[3] It is important to note that transformation occurs for the speaker and the listener.

Listening is a vital first step for communication. To cultivate our leadership life stories in the coming chapters, we will look back at the disciples' stories and listen to their personalities and characteristics. This will open opportunities to experience a glimpse of the Father, Son, and Holy Spirit, the perfect interaction of the Trinity.

Landmark Three: Leadership Equals Authentic Service and Co-created Meaning

Another landmark that helps provide direction is an understanding of leadership that focuses on authentic, servant-based leadership created through shared meaning. Definitions of leadership abound today. In fact, Bernard Bass's *Handbook of Leadership* observes that "there are almost as many different definitions of leadership as there are persons who have attempted to define the concept."[4]

But what if there were a way to see leadership a bit differently? That different view, introduced by Wilfred Drath and Charles Palus, signals an important shift toward a meaning-making perspective of leadership. To approach leadership as meaning making, an individual figures out why an event or process is important and then begins to frame this understanding within their organizations and communities. As noted in Drath and Palus's Center for Creative Leadership (CCL) report, leadership as meaning making comes from a constructivist view and "makes sense of an action by placing it within some larger frame."[5]

A meaning-making leadership perspective is also present in the concepts of servant leadership and authentic leadership. Robert Greenleaf was the first to coin the term servant leadership in the 1970s. His three foundational essays suggest ideas for the individual, the institution, and trustees. Authentic leadership surged in popularity in the early 2000s with work from theorists and practitioners. The four pillars of authentic leadership—self-awareness, relational transparency, balanced processing, and a strong moral code—help leaders and followers understand why events are important.[6] Both servant leadership and authentic leadership focus on the intentional work of leaders and followers working together toward a shared and co-constructed meaning.[7]

There is no need to provide you with a dissertation on leadership theory and practice. Thousands of pages have already been filled breaking down those ideas, but some can be useful in our discussion of leadership life stories. The landmark that provides direction here is the idea that effective leadership results from a meaning-making perspective—one in which leaders and followers co-create and work toward a shared meaning.

Landmark Four: Personal Growth from Solitude and Community

A fourth landmark to consider in cultivating leadership life stories is individual growth, nurtured both in solitude and in community. Northwestern University Professor Don McAdams explains how individuals search for and find human identity. In his book *Stories We Live By*, McAdams writes that "each of us comes to know who he or she is by creating a heroic story of the self."[8] As an individual develops, he or she reflects on and considers the personal life story.

Not only do individuals grow and engage their personal identity in thoughts and action by themselves, but they also engage identity as part of a community. Community groups, ranging from families to neighborhoods to churches to work and school, help the individual test and refine personal development. Jesus reached out and called each of the 12 disciples and for three years he worked with them as individuals and as a community to help them perceive their own leadership life stories. My hope is that the reader of this book will be enabled to use a similar model of cultivating leadership life stories, through time with self and time in a community.

Wrapping Up: Building Shalom in a Broken World

As we reflect on the mapping out of our journey, we should acknowledge that we live in a world broken by sin which affects us every day. Yet, the promise of shalom is that we can get a small taste of the perfect goodness of heaven. We can see these gifts of shalom through the process of leadership life stories. How are you seeing, feeling, and experiencing a small taste of heaven today? Perhaps a few examples from my own life will help you recognize moments of shalom in yours.

Professionally, most of my career has been with institutions that do not explicitly proclaim Christ. Even in these environments, Jesus is seen. Often, I'm one of the few people of faith that people see and interact with. Each day I have the opportunity to help learners make Jesus real in their lives.

Personally, I get the fresh breath of heaven in my lungs in some of the toughest times of life. Recently, a social media memory popped up depicting a flower in my front yard. The memory took me back to a very difficult time in my family life. At that time, everything bad was getting worse. Sitting on the front porch that day, feeling the weight of the world on my shoulders, I saw this red flower poking through a bed of silver weeds and thought, "Whew, I think I can take another step today." This one step became another and then another and then another. Shalom comes in the small moments of life, as the Holy Spirit brings a glimpse of the joy and peace of heaven to our broken world. This step of shalom can be both nervous and exciting when we fully give ourselves over to the call of Jesus in our lives.

Action Steps: Your Commitment to Move Forward

While an understanding of the 12 disciples is important, "scripture always keeps the focus on the power of Christ and the power of the Word, not the men who were merely instruments of that power. These men were filled with the Spirit and they preached the Word."[9] That same power is available through Jesus today. Here is the question: Are you ready to begin this journey? Here are action steps to take as you embark.

1. **Step One**. Commit your future movements to the Lord through prayer. Below is a suggested short prayer:

   Thank you, Jesus, for the free gift of salvation and your sacrifice on the cross. Lord, I know that you are here and actively involved in my life. As I begin these steps toward developing my leadership life story, help me feel the powerful movements and the gentle nudges of the Holy Spirit. In the days, weeks, and months to come, I give you all of the honor and glory. In the name of the Father, Son, and Holy Spirit, Amen.

2. **Step Two**. Find one or two people who can serve as your community during this journey. Meet with them or send them a quick note to let them know about the steps you'll be taking and the part they can play.

Our next step will be to look back at the leadership life stories of some Agents of Shalom. As we move forward toward building shalom, we'll consider how each first-century story lends wisdom to twenty-first century leaders.

Discussion Questions

1. As you consider leadership life stories, what are you most interested in or excited about?

2. What are some personal landmarks in your life? Why are these important to you?

3. Who are the two or three people you can engage as you take this journey?

4. Finish this sentence: I think leadership life stories can be most helpful to a leader by... ?

Chapter 2

James the Less: Life Stories Rooted in Christ

One of those days Jesus went out to a mountainside to pray, and spent the night praying to God. When morning came, he called his disciples to him and chose twelve of them, whom he also designated apostles: Simon (whom he named Peter), his brother Andrew, James, John, Philip, Bartholomew, Matthew, Thomas, James son of Alphaeus, Simon who was called the Zealot, Judas son of James, and Judas Iscariot, who became a traitor.

—Luke 6:12–16

THE JOURNEY TOWARD LEADERSHIP LIFE STORIES begins by understanding that all stories matter. To mine the depth of our stories for meaning, we must develop a foundation with deep roots that explore the hidden and peculiar treasures from our unique personalities. This chapter looks at the life of James the Less and defines leadership life stories. With knowledge of our life stories, as agents of shalom and with Christ as our compass, we find God's presence in everything. Then, as his presence permeates our leadership life stories, we can be used to point others back to the saving grace of Jesus Christ.

The meaning in our stories doesn't present itself in neon lights; often, it is just beneath the surface. When we dig in and brush off the unassuming ground cover, God's glory shines through. Our family visit to Mammoth Cave National Park in Kentucky reminds me of just this process. Mammoth Cave National Park is one of the largest cave systems in the world with over 400 miles of explored caverns and trails. The national park website calls Mammoth Cave a "grand, gloomy, and peculiar place." Each year, about half a million people explore the underground cavities of this natural wonder. Guided tours travel paths from a short quarter mile to hikes over five hours. Visitors brush by flowstones and dripstones or walk under stalactites and around stalagmites.[1]

The park was officially organized in 1941, but men of color played an important role in exploring the cave system as far back as the 1830s. These hidden stories, the pivotal leadership of these men, and the Bransford family connection were unearthed in a 2014 *New York Times* piece titled "In Kentucky, a Family at the Center of the Earth."[2] Jerry Bransford, a fifth-generation tour guide, led our family on this trip, walking us through his family stories and along the underground trails. His family history included Matt Bransford, a third-generation tour guide who estimated that he walked over 50,000 miles underground, and Mat (Materson) Bransford, who was one of the first explorers of the cave system. During our tour, the bus took a short detour to drive by the farmstead where the cabins housing the early families stood. While the frames of the houses are long gone, the foundations remain. Jerry Bransford intentionally leads his tours to this spot so that visitors hear stories that were almost lost to history.

Just like Jerry Bransford's story, our leadership life stories may lie just beneath the surface. These roots are built up in a relationship with Jesus Christ, are strengthened, and can overflow with grace and truth. We just need to make the choice and take the first step. As we consider James the Less, it is important to remember that in a world of choices, we are chosen by the Lord.

Calling the Disciples: James Son of Alphaeus

At the beginning of his ministry, Jesus Christ specifically selected 12 men who became his disciples. These were common men with an uncommon calling. In the New Testament, the disciples' names are listed three times (Matt. 10:2–4; Mark 3:16–19; Luke 6:14–16). Each of these scriptural passages list the disciples in descending order from the most intimate of Jesus to the least intimate. These individuals are sorted into three different groups, or tiers. Group One is Simon Peter, John, James the Greater, and Andrew; Group Two is Matthew, Nathanael, Philip, and Thomas; and Group Three is James the Less, Simon, Thaddeus, and Judas Iscariot. Professor of Theology and author W. Brian Shelton says "this should not suggest inferiority or a lesser kingdom contribution for the third tier but is only a group based on the extent of their recorded activity.[3] Regardless of where they show up in the order, it is important to remember that each of these men used their unique personalities through the power of the Holy Spirit to spread the Glory Story of Jesus Christ to the ends of the earth.

While we have varying amounts of information about each specific disciple, it should be noted that each disciple is an agent of shalom through his acceptance of the free gift of salvation. Each disciple responded to Jesus throughout his ministry on earth, and each of the disciples' leadership life stories became part of the overarching Glory Story of Jesus Christ.

Looking Back: The Story of James the Less

This book begins by examining the least-known disciple: James son of Alphaeus. In all of the lists, he is mentioned near the end. Although we may not know the exact stories or specific moments from the life of James, we do know that he was with Jesus during his ministry on earth. I sometimes think about this disciple and the three years he spent with the other disciples, learning at the feet of Jesus. Was James there when the water was turned into wine or when the paralytic man was lowered through the roof? What was his reaction and what did he say? We have no record of these things.

By looking within the Gospels, we may be able to make some assumptions about this disciple. In Mark 15:40 after the death of Jesus, James son of Alphaeus has a different nickname. At the crucifixion it says, "Some women were watching from a distance. Among them were Mary Magdalene, Mary the mother of James the younger and of Joseph and Solome" (Mark 15:40). The Greek word used here is *mikros* which can translate to English as "the less" or "little."[4] With *the Less* tacked onto the end of his name, my imagination goes to wondering if James may have been young or small in stature. This is an interesting thought to me because even the smallest, most insignificant stories can be used in the greater story of Jesus Christ.

Outside of the Gospels, there is some additional information. Scholars claim that James *the Less* may have made some significant decisions for the early church, as he, with other disciples, led an important meeting around 50 A.D.[5] The discussion centered on who could become followers of Jesus. James listened carefully to the disagreement and was a pivotal voice, saying that the free gift of salvation through Jesus was open to everyone. James the Less went on to proclaim salvation and bring others to the Lord.[6] While James the Less has no speaking parts in the Gospel, we do know that he was called by the Lord—and he was faithful to use his leadership life story in the overarching Glory Story of Jesus Christ.

Looking Forward: First-century Lessons for Twenty-first Century Leaders

When we consider first-century James the Less in light of our potential as leaders today, lessons rise to the surface. James the Less's life story is not explicitly documented in the Bible, but his name, his faithfulness, and his community among the disciples were still recognized by the Savior. For three years, James the Less traveled and had conversations with Jesus. Even though these moments are not recorded and we may not know the specifics of his interactions, we know they happened and were used by Jesus to be a part of the Glory Story.

As faithful communicators, our leadership life stories are important regardless of whether or not they are highlighted, reposted, or remembered beyond today. The very process of learning about and sharing our leadership life stories can nurture us spiritually while blessing those with whom we share community. Jesus asked the disciples to follow; he sought their faithfulness. Ultimately, Jesus knows the leadership life story of each individual. If we are faithful to engage others with what he has given us, then he weaves the tapestry that points to his glory.

Building Shalom: Called, Chosen, Faithful

Much like James the Less, we, too, are called out of obscurity and into faithfulness. Jesus communicates with us and pours into our lives. Jesus invites us to minister with him—to join him in community—as we make disciples of all nations, sharing a taste of the grace and peace of heaven along the way. Being people of shalom is not always easy, but "Jesus is the way of the shalom person."[7]

As we begin this journey of leadership life stories it is important to remember that all of the disciples left everything to follow Jesus. Christ asks us to do the same with our leadership life stories. May we embrace that opportunity today as agents of shalom.

Action Steps

You have a hidden and peculiar set of stories waiting just below the surface. In the next chapter, we will take steps to identify what happened in those stories so you can craft a message that begins to connect with others. These action steps will help you get ready for that process.

1. **Step One**. Jot down three personal moments that jumped out in your mind while reading this chapter. Any experience will work. The key to this action step is to begin thinking about the moments and the experiences that surround us each day.

2. **Step Two**. Start to listen well to those in your life and tune in to their leadership life stories. Think back to a specific conversation from this past week. Write down a few notes about this time spent with others. What was said? What did you learn? What did you think? How did you feel?

Discussion Questions

1. Name one thing you learned in this chapter about James the Less. How does this new information affect your thinking about leadership or leadership life stories?

2. If James was called James the Less and does not figure significantly into Scripture, how can you make a case for him as an individual with a leadership life story?

3. Begin thinking about some of the seemingly insignificant leadership moments in your life. What is the Holy Spirit bringing to your mind?

4. Can you think of and list times in your life where you were impacted by a leader? Briefly discuss these moments with your friend.

Chapter 3

Thaddeus: The Elements of Formative Moments

But Lord, why do you intend to show yourself to us and not to the world?

—John 14:22

WE EXPERIENCE MANY FORMATIVE MOMENTS in life. All these moments, both good and bad, can be part of our leadership life story. An important first step as agents of shalom is to discover the pivotal moments of our life stories. Several elements are necessary for this reflection process. It can take courage to reflect on the past, but we are not alone in this process, for the triune God is there to dialogue with us. Faithful communicators engage the interactive back and forth of the communication process, creating a sacred space that reflects the perfect shalom found in the interaction of Father, Son, and Holy Spirit. When we share our stories or listen to others' formative moments, we invite them into that sacred space. The process of sharing and listening cultivates another necessary element for leadership life stories: a tender heart.

This chapter builds on the hidden and peculiar moments you identified earlier. These pictures will help you identify specific formative or fortuitous moments of leadership, and along the way, you will have the opportunity to exercise and cultivate both courage and a tender heart.

Calling the Disciples: Thaddeus

Thaddeus is the disciple known by many names. In the list of the 12 disciples, his name is listed as: Thaddeus, Thaddaeus, Jude, Judas. His name has been translated to mean a person who is child-like or who has a tender heart. In some texts his last name, Labbeus, is also mentioned, which can mean courageous.[1] Through the brief picture of Thaddeus developed in John 14, we learn that Thaddeus was a man who had deep compassion for others; he desperately wanted everyone to know Christ.

Much like James the Less, there is very little biblical information about Thaddeus. His birthplace, his childhood, his connection and call to Jesus, and his specific action steps with Jesus are all lost to history. What we do know is that Thaddeus fully accepted the call to be an agent of shalom and to serve the rest of his life proclaiming Jesus as Lord and Savior. While we hear about Thaddeus in the books of Matthew, Mark, Luke, and Acts, his only speaking part is in John 14:22. There are two important items about this Bible verse that help us understand a bit about the personality of Thaddeus and the connection to leadership life stories—namely, Thaddeus has courage to speak up and interrupt Jesus, and Thaddeus reveals his tender heart for others.

Looking Back: The Story of Thaddeus

John 14 provides an interesting moment of courage for Thaddeus. This story comes immediately after Jesus washed the feet of the disciples and everyone was eating dinner. I imagine this was a serious dinner with little conversation. The disciples, though, probably pushed and shoved each other for the place of honor next to Jesus. As Jesus breaks bread and drinks wine during the Passover Feast, connecting the upcoming crucifixion to their salvation, glances of frustration might have been exchanged among the 12 as some struggled to understand. Were the disciples lost in their own thoughts, or did they stare with confusion at the roof?

Jesus speaks for a while, and then Thomas asks a question. After Jesus answers, Philip throws out a question of his own. Jesus answers and explains to the disciples what is coming. In reading this chapter, it appears that by verse 22, the time for questions is over. Jesus launches into an explanation of what they and he must do. Yet in the middle of this pivotal moment, as Jesus pours out his heart to the disciples, Thaddeus interrupts with the words, "Lord, why do you intend to show yourself to us and not the world?" (John 14:22).

I believe that Thaddeus was one of the disciples who tracked every action step Jesus took and every word he said. I can imagine this rush of words pouring from Thaddeus's mouth while tears slip from his eyes, showing us that, at least, he saw the seriousness of the supper. Even at this important time and place, Thaddeus had the courage to interrupt Jesus. Even in this rush of words, Thaddeus displays a tender heart for others. Thaddeus already recognizes that the Glory Story to be accomplished by

Christ would be available to everyone. While the full impact of the death and resurrection of Jesus was yet to be seen during this verse, Thaddeus already recognizes the perfect shalom—the peace, unity, and community—found in Christ. In the next few verses in John 14, Jesus gently reminds Thaddeus that only those who accept the free gift of salvation will receive an inheritance in the Kingdom of God.

This brief back and forth between Thaddeus and Jesus in John 14 provides an example for faithful communicators who serve as agents of shalom. Leadership life stories developed in courage and shared with a tender heart can give this broken world a glimpse of the joy to come as seen through the perfect unity of Father, Son, and Holy Spirit.

Fundamentals of Leadership Life Stories

We began by identifying several formative and fortuitous moments of life. When we think back through these pivotal moments, we see a picture in our mind's eye of that place and time. Think back to the moments you have identified so far. How can they connect to what you may have learned about the process of leadership or how did something from the event improve your practice of leadership? These times could be an event, an action, or a simple conversation or quote that stays with you. Perhaps it involved someone who is an important leader in your life? Maybe the leadership moments in your life involved a specific sports team, an organization, or a community, and developed over a few weeks or months? Several leadership principles and examples can help you begin to identify these moments.

Leadership Principle: Courage

There is a wonderful word in the Icelandic language that helps us as we take this important first step: *kjarkur*. While there is no direct translation to the English language, *kjarkur* most closely connects to the idea of courage. In English, courage means a gut-level bravery in situations. The Nordic understanding adds a level of intensity: *kjarkur* is a deep, gutsy sense of purpose and action.[2] *Kjarkur*, in the context of leadership life stories, reminds us of the courage needed as we, each day, have the choice to interact with others. In this interaction, we engage with our life story, contributing alongside others to our continued development.

One of my leadership life stories revolves around the need for courage. It begins in a hospital bed with a syringe of pork insulin. I remember going to the doctor's office to get my blood sugar tested when I was thirteen years old. I was having trouble keeping on weight. I was always thirsty and as a result, awoke multiple times a night to go to the bathroom. My breath smelled fruity, which I later learned was a symptom of ketoacidosis. The doctor put all these clues together, determining that my pancreas did not secrete insulin. I was diagnosed with Type 1 diabetes. A key picture in my mind shows me sitting in the hospital bed, learning how to measure the proper amount of insulin in a syringe to stay healthy. I practiced giving insulin shots to grapefruits and oranges to get the feel of doing that same thing to my body. Today, due to advances in medicine, I wear an insulin pump and check my blood sugar multiple times a day.

My decades-long journey as a diabetic is one of my leadership life stories. This diagnosis is an important formative moment in my life—one that includes both challenges and victories. A challenging aspect of this story is that I endure the shots, the blood tests, and the swings from high blood sugar to low blood sugar, every day. At the beginning, as a thirteen-year-old boy, it took courage for me to accept the fact that my life would never be normal and that I would have to count the cost whenever I ate out. Now, when people ask, my courage has been strengthened and it is easier to share both the challenges and the victories.

Leadership Principle: Listening with a Tender Heart

My life as a Type 1 diabetic has not only nurtured courage, but it has also taught me other methods for communicating faithfully. Others listened to me along the way, and this has helped me see the value of listening and being more tenderhearted toward others who are going through personal health challenges. The value of listening was also emphasized early in my media career when I was required to attend a full-day training session to learn how to listen. This was frustrating for me. I figured that as a reporter, my primary job was to speak and get information out to the public for consumption. I was surprised to see that this session turned my world upside down.

The morning was spent learning about the good practice of hearing. We discussed principles like the importance of eye contact, nonverbal feedback, providing empathy, and others. That morning I thought, "These are important, but they do not relate to my job." The afternoon centered on the phenomena of listening. Building from the skills of the morning, we drilled down to why we engage another person. I realized in that session that everyone has a dynamic and unique story. This training session was a fortuitous moment that reordered my mindset of communication and leadership; suddenly, listening was first in importance. When we, as faithful communicators, truly hear another person as they speak, we are displaying a tender heart—one that puts others first.

Looking Forward: From Pictures to Formative Moments to Shalom

The formative moments of leadership are all around us. Think through the key turning points of your life. These are usually made of formative moments (e.g., a promotion at work or leading in a family situation) or a fortuitous experience (e.g., a short conversation with a friend, listening to a speech, or the change experienced in an unexpected situation). As you reflect on your experiences, remember that formative and fortuitous moments share two qualities: they disrupt the journey and they provide a turning point in our leadership communication.

On a recent trip to Charleston, South Carolina, a centuries-old photograph reminded me of the power the visual holds and how it can lead us to shalom. After a busy academic year, exploring this city was a welcome break. One of the days was spent wandering around the Magnolia Plantation and Gardens. The King of England gifted the Drayton family this land in 1676. There were some battles during the Revolutionary War (1775–1783) and skirmishes during the Civil War (1860s). The Gardens opened in the 1870s and are the oldest public gardens in the United States.[3] We had a wonderful few hours touring and learning about the good and flawed history of this place.

What struck me, though, was a simple picture located back on the natural trails along the Ashley River. This picture, taken in the 1850s by Matthew Brady, is one of the earliest known photos in the country. It depicts the Reverend John Grimke Drayton with his granddaughter. At the time, Reverend Drayton was an important figure not only in the church but in the social world of South Carolina.[4] The picture of Reverend Drayton with his granddaughter appears to be a routine trip around the back trails of the plantation, perhaps a familiar activity for them. This picture disrupted my thinking that day and reminded me of something important; it was a formative moment for me. I realized that pictures can provide a window to our soul that helps us develop a tender heart.

I remember gazing at that simple picture that day, and my imagination saw a smile on the pastor's face as his granddaughter twirls around the path, investigating the flowers and insects. The heavy, humid air breezes through the rice fields and reeds. I had the sense that the pastor often sat in this secluded place to listen to the Word of God, plan his sermons, and enjoy time with his granddaughter. I believe that the Reverend Drayton intentionally came to this place because this was a place where he had a tender heart. The scene depicts shalom. There is harmony and peace in a place where God is met as King, Jesus as Shepherd, and the Holy Spirit as Comforter. The picture also increases my desire for shalom. As a faithful communicator, I want to experience shalom and I want to share it with others.

Building Shalom by Being Quiet

Courage is required to be reflective. To look at past moments, we have to sift through the sad and happy moments, the uncomfortable and awkward ones. It also takes courage to listen to others, for we are voluntarily entering into another person's space. Annette Simmons writes in *The Story Factor* that "genuine listening has a deep, transformative power."[5] That transformation occurs for both the speaker and the listener. By the end of the mandatory session I attended, I had experienced my own transformative moment through listening. I also realized that others could connect to the power that is found in moments of quiet. When we listen rather than speak, we give the individual who is speaking a place of prominence. When we listen, we hold another person's trust carefully. When we listen, we show humility.

I have been blessed to listen to stories from all sorts of individuals. I have celebrated professional success in baseball clubhouses with athletes and in boardrooms with entrepreneurs. I have cultivated a tender heart as I have cried and groaned in grief in my personal life and in the lives of others. The transformative power of leadership life stories begins when we listen. Listening is at the heart of building shalom.

Just as Thaddeus was identified by many names, we may be identified by several leadership life stories. Thaddeus is called the Patron Saint for Hopeless or Lost Causes. He courageously preached the gospel in some of the most difficult situations for the early church. Pray that God will give you strength to engage the challenges and victories of life as you reflect on the past and forward toward the coming journey, on the way to shalom for yourself and others.

> Lord, as we continue to identify the formative and fortuitous moments of our leadership life stories, please send the help of the Holy Spirit so that we can engage the good and challenging moments of our lives with courage and a tender heart. In Jesus's name, Amen.

Action Steps

In our visual culture, it is estimated that each person takes 10 to 12 pictures a day with their cell phones. In a 24-hour time period, trillions of pictures and videos are taken by the world's eight billion people. We take pictures because we want to remember the important moments of our lives. My mobile is filled with quick shots on vacation, get-togethers with friends, and events or items I want to remember. I challenge you to use a picture to identify the top five specific formative or fortuitous moments that provide the starting point of your leadership life stories. Remember that at this point, we are focused on discovering what happened in your pictures and identifying the moment.

1. **Step One**. Scroll through your pictures and find five to ten pictures that are important to you. Look for pictures that provide a memorable moment. At the time of that picture—or looking back at it now—how did you learn about an aspect of leadership?

2. **Step Two**. Consider each picture individually. Stay focused on the moment from the picture; remember the time, the place, and the people. Begin to think about the sights, sounds, smells of this time. Write down all you can remember about the thoughts, feelings, and impressions of that moment.

These last two chapters have led us to think about the hidden and peculiar stories and pictures that make up your unique leadership life stories. Hopefully, you have been able to find a few significant pictures, identify the formative and/or fortuitous moments of your life, and consider what happened. In this process, much of the focus has been on you in that moment. Let's step outside that moment to consider how this process can build bridges to those around us.

Discussion Questions

1. Most of us associate courage with a leader, but a tender heart is a less expected leadership quality. Do you agree with that statement?

2. Think of a time when being quiet made the difference in a leadership situation. Describe that situation and explain how quiet helped lead to shalom.

3. List your thoughts on how to balance the virtues of courage and a tender heart in leadership.

4. In what ways do you think telling and listening to stories help to build trust and authenticity in leadership?

Chapter 4

Simon the Zealot:
Commitment and Participation

Then Jesus said to his disciples, "Whoever wants to be my disciple must deny themselves and take up their cross and follow me. For whoever wants to save their life will lose it, but whoever loses their life for me will find it."

—Matthew 16:24

SOON AFTER GRADUATING WITH MY DEGREE in communication, I found myself interviewing athletes on and off the field. I learned from their stories about their failures and successes. I learned what it takes to get to the top and play professional baseball, football, and hockey. I still pay attention to the time and commitment it takes for athletes to be the best. One professional athlete stands above all others, NBA player Kobe Bryant. This generational talent played his entire 20-year career with the Los Angeles Lakers.

Kobe made headlines for his dedication to basketball and his health. For example, later in his career after tearing his Achilles tendon, he returned to the lineup and was back on the court just eight months after the injury. The typical recovery time can be as long as 18 months. Kobe displayed an unwavering devotion to working out, sometimes as early as 3:00 AM, doing three-a-day practice sessions. He would even stay at practice until he hit 400 shots.[1]

I think about this level of focus in professional sports when we turn our attention to Simon the Zealot. In all the Gospel narratives, Simon is described as a Zealot. Scholars are not sure if the zealousness was because of his personality or because of his religious zeal and the radical Zealot party. While we have few clues in Scripture, what we can conclude is that Simon is probably a high emotional and high intensity individual. When he commits, Simon is all in and over the top. Jesus, however, shifts Simon's purpose from an earthly kingdom to an eternal one. Simon, after spending time with Jesus, began to share Jesus's mission; he understood *why* he was committed. This chapter takes the formative and fortuitous leadership moments identified earlier (*what* happened) and begins to develop an understanding about *why* these leadership life stories are important.

Through the life of Simon the Zealot, we realize that leadership life stories take commitment and intensity. Our leadership life stories not only explain who we are, they can also set a goal for who we want to be. These stories also link us to others; through the process of communication, shared meaning connects people across cultures and around the globe.

Calling the Disciples: Simon the Zealot

Simon is another disciple we only hear about when his name is listed in the Gospels (Matt. 10:2–4; Mark 3:16–19; and Luke 6:12–16). As a quick reminder: Simon the Zealot is not Simon Peter; he will be discussed later. Jesus reaches out to Simon the Zealot and personally calls him to ministry, but the specific time or place is never recorded. When he is called by Jesus in the Gospels, Simon is always called Simon the Zealot. It appears that Simon was strongly committed to thought and action. The Zealot is a descriptive phrase that stuck with him during his time with Jesus and even after the resurrection as he further testified about salvation through Jesus Christ. We can conclude that, throughout the Gospel narratives, he likely remains a high commitment, high emotion, and high intensity individual. Simon, after spending time with Jesus, began to share Jesus's mission; he understood why he was committed. This chapter takes the formative and fortuitous leadership moments identified earlier and begins to develop an understanding about why these leadership life stories are important.

Looking Back: The Story of Simon the Zealot

Simon is an extremist in every sense. The Zealots were a political group that used any means possible to get the Roman Empire out of the Holy Land. The Zealot movement began with a rebellion in 7 A.D. after an unfair tax was forced on the people by the Roman government. The story of the Zealots is filled with secret meetings, back-room deals, and murder. The specific group in the area at this time had arisen to overthrow Roman rule. Zealots took matters into their own hands and did what they felt needed to be done. This included stabbing Roman soldiers to try and start violent uprisings. By the time Jesus began his ministry, Zealots had no problem killing Romans as a form of protest.[2]

Simon is sometimes associated with Judas Iscariot, the traitor.[3] Some think that Simon and Judas Iscariot both came from an extremist position. Perhaps these men began as disciples of Jesus because they hoped for an earthly revolution against the Roman government.[4] During their time with Jesus, however, the stories of Simon and Judas Iscariot took very different paths. While Judas became a traitor, Simon became an evangelizer. His zealous characteristics and extreme views for rebellion on earth shifted to a heavenly kingdom. Simon accepted the free gift of salvation and fundamentally changed his core purpose toward the Glory Story. Simon was someone with "fierce loyalties, amazing passion, courage, zeal."[5] Simon accepted the truth and acknowledged Christ as his Lord. The passionate zeal he once held for Israel was now channeled into his dedication to Christ.

I wonder about the private conversations that took place as Jesus, Simon, and others traveled from town to town. What did Jesus say that helped Simon understand the gospel? What did Simon see that shifted his focus from hurting the Romans to healing people with the good news of the gospel? While these interactions are never noted in Scripture, it is clear that the ultimate Glory Story was revealed to Simon. He learned the core message of his leadership life story and entered into a shared meaning through his communication with Jesus.

Leadership Life Stories as a Shared Process

Leadership is more than just an event and a means of influence. Leadership is developed in and comes out of the communication process. Robert Greenleaf's servant leadership concept, mentioned earlier, reveals an effective mix of communication and leadership. His first three essays, written in the early 1970s, provide a framework for others to work from in their own spheres of influence.[6] Fifty years later, some reject the concept because it seems weak; however, I believe that the attitudes and actions of servant leadership emerge from personal and emotional strength. The intensity and commitment to the present in servant leadership impacts leaders and followers. Leadership life stories start from an understanding of communication, and some theories and models can aid in that understanding. The understanding of leadership as a shared process is clarified as we now consider several well-researched leadership principles.

Leadership Principle: The Value of the Past, Present, and Future

Not only is communication a shared process between individuals, but it is affected by a shared sense of the past, the present, and the future. Communication theorist Frank Dance offers a helical model of human communication, shaped like a tornado that spirals up and expands with each communication event. Dance says that "the communication process, like the helix, is constantly moving forward and yet is always to some degree dependent upon the past, which informs the present and the future."[7] Today's communication pushes toward tomorrow and is dependent upon past communication. In other words, present and future communication have both been informed and are influenced by past communication. Without a shared sense of the past, present, and future, our uninformed communication can fall short of accomplishing its purpose.

A personal example may help to develop this idea. As I write these words, my wife and I have been married for just over one year. When dating, we reached a point where three significant words could be said: "I love you." Thinking about the newness of the relationship, saying "I love you" was an important moment. When I said "I love you" and had a ring, another level was engaged. This is a second marriage for both of us, so there are added challenges as a blended family. As we navigate the bumps and bruises of our earlier failed attempts and as we approach middle age and a blended family, "I love you" has many meanings. Each time I look into the eyes of my bride, I need to understand that all of the years of "I love you" from the past influence the understanding of this moment of saying "I love you." Each "I love you" that I say is based on hearing "I love you" from the people in our lives, past and present. This helical model of communication with its appreciation of past, present, and future can provide a framework in our discussion of leadership life stories.

Leadership Principle: The Value of Stories for Shared Meaning

Just as the past, present, and future merge in the communication of meaning, shared stories can result in shared meaning. Communication professor Walter Fisher is another author who provides a framework that may help as we engage the process of leadership life stories. Fisher offers the idea that as humans we create and understand meaning through a narrative or storytelling process. He suggests that stories "offer an approach to interpretation and assessment of human communication."[8] Stories provide an opportunity to create a shared meaning. When we engage this process, a new level of intensity and commitment emerges as we begin to understand why the moments in our stories are important to us and possibly to others. We commit to our purpose more fully when we begin to understand the meaning in our life stories. We begin to see those stories as steps on the path to leadership.

Leadership Principle: The Community Effect of Personal Shared Meaning

Wilfred Drath and Charles Palus note in a Center for Creative Leadership report that meaning making in leadership "makes sense of an action by placing it within some larger frame."[9] When we seek shared meaning in the communication process, we seek to reveal the perfect peace and goodness that can only be found in Jesus Christ. Our stories constantly evolve, change, and grow, yet as faithful communicators, each of these stories rests on a solid foundation of faith and the redeeming work of salvation seen in the Glory Story.

Looking Forward: First-century Commitment and Participation Reimagined

It is interesting that Jesus selects someone like Simon to be part of his closely trusted disciples. Jesus took the fiery personality and gung-ho attitude of Simon to grow the early church. An amazing and radical transformation shifted the earthly focus to a heavenly meaning in his life. Just as he did with Simon the Zealot, Jesus can redirect our passion toward his purpose. Commitment speaks volumes to those around us, encouraging them to share with others. As we communicate faithfully, past and present merge, compelling us toward the future. Our attempt to connect with others and create shared meaning through our leadership life stories helps us uncover what is important to us but can also guide others toward a shared meaning in families, communities, and organizations.

Building Shalom by Sharing Stories

At eye level behind my computer is a yellow sticky note. In black bold print, there is part of a quote from T. S. Eliot's poem, "The Dry Salvages": "We had the *experience* but missed the *meaning*."[10] I have italicized the two words in the quote because I wonder if there are times that we focus so much on the practice of leading others that we miss the personal meaning of the moment. As faith-filled communicators, it is important for us to be obedient to the direction and nudges of the Holy Spirit. A shift toward the shared meaning developed within leadership life stories can elevate meaning over experience. When we share our leadership life stories and listen to the leadership life stories of others, we engage in a meaning-centered focus that cultivates our personal and professional lives and the lives of others.

For me, coffee is an important element to developing shared meaning with others. A former professor of mine often said, "Coffee is the visible sign that God loves us." During my work with state government, I was responsible for the training and development of over 200 phone operators in a call center. During the full-day training event, it was important for me to have hot coffee available. Then the dreaded letter came from leadership. There was no more money available in the training budget for this frivolous expense.

I began to make my own purchases, buying ground coffee and fixings for those attending training events. Not only was the caffeine important to get us going in the morning, but coffee time encouraged conversation as people entered the room. Weeks after training sessions were completed, people I had helped train would return, unpaid, and we would sit and talk about life and their work over cups of coffee. Many of these conversations stayed professional and focused on the job, but some of them also turned personal. I heard about the joys of new babies and family members, questions about continuing with the work, and even the challenges of some of the phone calls the individuals had fielded.

The cup of coffee became not just a shot of caffeine to stay awake during a long day of training, but it provided a bridge to shared meaning through the highs and lows of life. I continued my personal leadership and used my personal budget for coffee for the next two years until I moved on to my next job at the university. During my final lunch at the call center, I was presented with two brand new coffee mugs. These are symbols for me, representing the importance of communication and the process of shared meaning that can develop through storytelling.

There are several extra-biblical stories about Simon after the Resurrection. The most dramatic is that Simon travelled to Persia and was sawed in half.[11] We may not know his final steps, but we do know that whatever happened, Simon the Zealot moved with high intensity and high commitment.

Jesus saw Simon's supposed character flaws as something he could use as he helped Simon develop a shared meaning focused on the Glory Story.

We recognize that we live in a difficult and challenging world. While this chapter has helped us understand the high moments of our leadership life stories, all around us lay broken stories. As agents of shalom, we have a choice every moment, even the moments that result in broken leadership life stories.

Action Steps

To help reveal your shared meaning, take the pictures from the earlier chapter and sit with them. As you follow the steps below, write down a few answers as the thoughts continue and your leadership life story develops. Remember that Simon reimagined his leadership, directing his passion toward the gospel. He discerned the why behind the moment. The goal of these next steps is to understand why your leadership moment is important. With these pictures in front of you, answer these questions:

1. What made the moment in this picture possible? Think about the environment, the situations, and your time in life.

2. How does this picture relate to your leadership experience? Who are the people in this moment, and what was the place in which this leadership moment occurred?

3. Looking at the pictures you collected, are there any common themes or patterns that emerge? How do these match up with your leadership vision and perspectives?

Take an additional step and reach out to those individuals in your community who you asked to partner with you on this leadership life story journey. Set up a time to talk this week over a cup of coffee or on a video chat. Engage a conversation about why these moments are important to you and how they formed your leadership.

Discussion Questions

1. Can you think of a time when a zealous nature or a bit too high intensity hindered your effectiveness as a leader?

2. Have you seen the effects of misdirected commitment in a leader? What happened and what do you think you have learned from this?

3. What are three of your initial thoughts about balancing a zealous, enthusiastic attitude and leading your team and family?

4. Where and how do you find peace to balance your zealous nature?

Chapter 5

Judas Iscariot:
Broken Leadership Life Stories

"Why wasn't this perfume sold and the money given to the poor?
It was worth a year's wages." He did not say this because he cared
about the poor but because he was a thief; as keeper of the money
bag, he used to help himself to what was put into it.

—John 12:5–6

As we develop the formative and fortuitous moments that make up
our leadership life stories, it is important to remember that individuals can
have similar experiences and similar situations yet have different results.
Hearts are softened or hardened; new journeys are explored or old habits
hidden. In the cases of Simon the Zealot and Judas Iscariot, we can see the
diverging paths of leadership life stories.

It appears that Judas Iscariot and Simon the Zealot came from a similar
background. In the beginning, both Judas and Simon sought action. They
were both driven by zeal to make things happen. It is assumed by some
Bible scholars that Simon the Zealot and Judas Iscariot were often sent out
as a pair to disciple and minister together.[1] Perhaps they were paired up
because they had similar thoughts, perspectives, and characteristics, but
ultimately, those yielded radically different results. Simon the Zealot was
open to the light of the truth in front of him, despite the broken path; Judas
chose to turn away from that truth. The difference in their leadership life
stories may help us understand how to engage not only our broken stories
but also the brokenness of those around us.

Calling the Disciples: Judas Iscariot

Judas Iscariot is the traitor. In all the lists of the disciples, Judas Iscariot is
listed last. Many times in Scripture he is identified as "the traitor" (Luke
6:16) or the one who "betrayed him" (Matt. 10:4). His failure to see the
Good News right in front of him has followed his story to the present day.

It is significant for us to remember that even though Jesus knew what Judas was doing, he still washed Judas's feet. Judas chose the wrong path, clearly. We are surrounded by choices in the world today, but even more significant than the temporal choices around us is a truth for us to remember: we are chosen by Jesus and offered the free gift of salvation and eternal life. Each individual has the choice to follow Christ or to take another path. Even our broken choices, however, do not stop the will of the Lord. Broken stories can be redeemed and used in the Glory Story. Jesus Christ can use even our missteps for his honor and glory.

Looking Back: The Story of Judas Iscariot

The question of why Judas Iscariot betrayed Jesus has no easy answer. Was he tempted because of money, power, or influence? One scholar suggested that "the evil action of Judas, like all human evil, was not foreordained but came as a result of wrong choices."[2] In John 12:4–6, it appears that Judas Iscariot followed Christ out of a desire for selfish gain. In this incident, Mary takes a pint of very expensive perfume and pours it over the feet of Jesus. Immediately Judas Iscariot complains, suggesting that the perfume should have been sold and the money given to the poor. Scripture tells us that Judas "did not say this because he cared about the poor but because he was a thief; as keeper of the money bag, he used to help himself to what was put into it" (John 12:6). Jesus sees right through the deception; of course, he knows that Judas helps himself to the funds. The most disgusting aspect of this is the verbal manipulation Judas practices, complaining that the money should be "given to the poor" as he tries to hide his theft. We can assume that, with this dark cloud already hovering over Judas, this small but open rebuke from Jesus might have turned Judas even further against Christ. The heart of Judas never changed. It appears that the light of truth only hardened him.

Limping Leadership with Its Bumps and Bruises

There are times in life when we miss the meaning right in front of us. Especially in broken moments, we often are not attuned to the truth. Judas Iscariot's story reminds us that the Lord always offers grace and forgiveness through the Glory Story if we will just accept him. He is the truth that stands before us. Unfortunately, many don't accept him, as we see in Judas Iscariot's story. It is true that we are all prone to sin. We all make choices that distance us from Jesus Christ. It is only through God's grace and the redeeming work of Jesus Christ that our leadership life stories can make a difference in our families, our work, and our communities. God can still use broken leadership life stories.

"Leadership with a limp" is a phrase I heard in conversation recently. This term, which can be traced back to John Wimber of the Vineyard Churches in the 1970s, has also been used by authors and speakers in the past few decades.[3] As agents of shalom, we can use the bumps and bruises of broken leadership life stories to engage others and to nurture shalom. One particular story comes to mind that exemplifies this idea.

The main character in this story had a deep drive for material and personal success. He gained victories through manipulation, hostility, and aggression. Years of this behavior followed him as he moved from town to town. The pressure and anxiety continued to grow almost to a breaking point. One night, all of his past seemed to climax in the present. Alone and isolated with nothing but the night sky, he suddenly faced an unknown opponent in hand-to-hand combat. Early in the contest, his hip was twisted out of the socket. In great pain, he continued wrestling until early dawn when the opponent left. This epic showdown became a formative experience for this individual, but for the rest of his life he walked with a limp. You may recognize this main character as Jacob from Genesis chapter 32 but you can also see its timeless quality as you look at culture today.

Leadership Principle: Limping Leadership as an Emotional Reminder

Limping leadership is a personal reminder of the emotional impact from pivotal leadership experiences. Jacob was emotionally changed through his experience, his identity shifting from an external focus to an eternal relationship.

I remember being encouraged into a leadership opportunity at a time in my life when I did not feel ready. At that stage of my life, I was juggling new family responsibilities at home and confidence issues in my mind, and this kept me from taking the last step to apply for an opportunity to facilitate work team discussions. Kevin, my team leader, emotionally supported me, listened to my questions, and walked side-by-side with me through the selection process. I can only assume that Kevin saw something in me that needed to be nurtured through this opportunity. Armed with training, I stepped into the new world of facilitation and my spiritual gift of teaching was unlocked. Part of the legacy of this book stems back to my team leader and his emotional encouragement.

This limping leadership experience strengthened me as a leader, and it serves as an emotional reminder for me. I learned about listening well, gently guiding people, and encouraging them until they gain the confidence to take steps on their own. I use a similar style of leadership as I nurture shalom in the classroom today.

Leadership Principle: Limping Leadership as a Physical Reminder

Limping leadership can also be a physical reminder to an individual. Jacob walked with a limp for the rest of his life. But consider how God can use this leadership limp as a visible reminder to others of the formative experience. In the case of Jacob, others may have seen his limp and a level of meaning was created between them; they likely considered the impact of the formative experience. For Jacob, this formative experience changed his communication with others and the broken relationship began to heal.

The concept of limping leadership helps us to see how the limp itself can be a blessing. Some of the writing about leadership with a limp seems to suggest that limps come out of weakness. I think limps, when viewed as physical reminders, can also become some of the greatest strengths. Earlier, I shared a formative experience of my diagnosis as a diabetic over thirty years ago. The insulin pump I wear on my hip every day is a physical reminder of this formative experience. Every day I see the pump as I plug in insulin to cover my food intake. Emotionally, I have learned the value of patience, persistence, and an added level of vulnerability.

Over the decades of shots, blood tests, and daily maintenance, I hope that I have developed a greater attitude of servant leadership. I have had to humbly ask forgiveness from friends and family for things I said while my blood sugar was low. While it has been a challenge, this formative experience has been an amazing blessing. I have found, just as Jacob did, that leadership life stories contain emotional and physical reminders of limping leadership; these reminders speak to us and to those around us.

Looking Forward: Engaging the Broken Pieces

As we look forward and mine lessons from the past for twenty-first century leaders, the story of Rotterdam, Netherlands, serves as a modern example. This city exemplifies the idea that leadership life stories can be redefined through tumultuous times, yielding the opportunity for new beginnings. Sitting near the west coast of Europe, this area in South Holland has settlements tracing back to 900 AD. Development continued through history with a strong maritime emphasis in the sixteenth and seventeenth centuries. This steady development of shipping and trade continued up to the 1940s.[4]

During World War II, however, Rotterdam was flattened. Locals in the area say that no event in the history of this city left a deeper scar. The medieval heart of the city was almost destroyed. A basic plan to redesign the city was initially much criticized but was eventually implemented. What could be saved from before the war was rebuilt, and what could not be saved was redesigned. This process continued with adjustments throughout the 1970s and 1980s. Today the city is known for innovative architecture, a modern skyline, and a city center that continues to grow.[5]

In situations like Rotterdam, how do leadership life stories engage the scar that is left? How do leadership life stories help individuals who are left feeling flattened and destroyed? I would like to suggest three ideas to help faithful communicators engage in broken leadership life stories. To remember these ideas, I'm going to suggest the ABCs: **A**djust thinking, **B**ase stories on shared meaning, and **C**reate a vision.

Adjust Thinking

Leadership life stories are most effective when they provide space for us to adjust our thinking and our actions. In the face of brokenness, we tend to avoid, but adjustments happen when we engage with broken leadership life stories. It is important for communities and individuals to sort through the process when rebuilding or redesigning. When engaging individuals with broken leadership life stories, remember that there are some who may decide to walk away.

In the case of Rotterdam there was initial criticism, but the community ultimately decided to save some of the pre-war neighborhoods while also building new neighborhoods and communities. The old and destroyed places add a level of character and understanding that informs the new. Adjusted thinking resulted in a stronger city and community.

Base Stories on Shared Meaning and Vision

Leadership life stories are most effective when they are based on an overarching story of meaning. The city of Rotterdam chose to join the past and present into their story for tomorrow. The overarching story of my life rests on my faith. My leadership life story is developed through my personal relationship with Jesus Christ. It is through the unchanging truth of the resurrection and saving grace of God that I can find meaning in the confusing times of destruction.

Leadership life stories are most effective when they provide vision. In the case of Rotterdam, the rebuilding process after World War II was not easy. In the initial stages, there was complaints, and there were tough questions that needed to be answered. Spending the time to listen and understand the variety of concerns voiced by groups and individuals is vital. A vision, a cooperative way forward, can help fuse the broken pieces.

Building Shalom by Engaging the Broken Pieces

We act as agents of shalom when we choose to engage even broken leadership life stories. And with the ability God has given us, we can discern the truth that is right in front of us. As faithful communicators, we have the opportunity to reflect a piece of the perfect shalom found in heaven even as we live in a broken world. Taking the step through pictures and moments to discover the hidden, peculiar leadership life stories in our lives allows us to reflect on what happened and why this is important to us. With this understanding, we can sift through moments that reflect brokenness and redeem them.

Action Steps

Broken leadership life stories surround us as individuals, communities, and organizations. As faithful communicators, we realize that broken leadership life stories can still be redeemed; they can contribute to the overarching Glory Story of Jesus Christ. If the broken leadership life story of Judas Iscariot teaches us anything we can remember that "out of evil God often brings good, as he did in the case of the traitor."[6]

The steps below can help you look critically at the moments you identified earlier, revealing not only tough lessons but also how those lessons can strengthen your leadership.

1. **Step One**. Going back to the moments you identified in the earlier chapter, what are some of the tough lessons you learned?

2. **Step Two**. How did the moments you identified change you, emotionally?

3. **Step Three**. What physical reminders do you carry from your broken leadership stories? How have those been redeemed?

4. **Step Four**. Write down three items that the Lord has redeemed through your broken leadership life stories.

Discussion Questions

1. Can you think of a broken situation that has been redeemed? It may be one similar to the city of Rotterdam or it could be something personal.

2. How can a leadership life story provide vision? Explain what this means to you.

3. What are three important steps a leader can take to help repair the broken stories we encounter each day?

4. Can broken leadership life stories still point back to the perfect goodness of heaven and shalom? How?

Section Two

MODELS OF SHALOM

Chapter 6

Nathanael: Leadership Life Stories of Self-awareness

"Nazareth! Can anything good come from there?" Nathanael asked. "Come and see," said Philip.

—John 1:46

"How do you know me?" Nathanael asked. Jesus answered, "I saw you while you were still under the fig tree before Phillip called you."

—John 1:48

WE ALL HAVE THOSE MOMENTS WHEN we open our mouths and speak before we think. Nathanael's negative thoughts spilled out in his words and were reclaimed through his leadership life story of self-awareness. I remember a personal moment of self-awareness and the humble character that was formed from one angry email. Working in state government as a training and development specialist at a remote call center site, I had over 200 people in and out of the office every day. Additionally, our central office often sent directives to help each of the remote sites stay on track and deliver consistent results.

I received an email late one afternoon after a busy day. It was from my colleague in another city and provided some direction and feedback on my recent training event. I shot back a quick, sarcastic, and tone-deaf reply to my colleague; it was a poor choice. I told her my exact feelings and hit send before thinking and before reviewing my written words.

The phone rang less than ten minutes later. Our boss Dorothy was on the line. Her direct, specific, and firm comments told me where I was off base. She strongly suggested that the tone of my written message should be corrected moving forward. I called my offended colleague, apologized for my behavior, and immediately took my corrective measures. Thankfully, Pam was gracious at this moment. The toughest part of this event for me was the embarrassment. Riding home after work, I could not escape the feeling of shame at letting my friends and colleagues down with my sarcastic comments. The words escaped my fingers before I engaged my brain.

Models of shalom are templates of past leaders that offer ideas to modern leaders moving forward. These examples can be powerful for us to understand how God continues his work in our lives as we continue our journey as agents of shalom. In the Bible, such stories are treasured and remembered.[1] This chapter explains how leadership life stories of self-awareness are developed in solitude and community. In addition, we see how effective leadership life stories are framed in a specific time that describes the moments.

Calling the Disciples: Nathanael

In our continuing life journeys, we make a choice to follow one path or the other. Similarly, early in the book of John, Nathanael finds himself at a pivotal time in life and receives the strength of Jesus Christ. Nathanael/ Bartholomew is from Cana in Galilee. While he is called Nathanael in the Book of John, all the other books of the Bible list him as Bartholomew.

There is some thought that Nathanael is considered his first name, while Bartholomew is generally considered his last name.[2] In this book, the name Nathanael will be used. We do not know about Nathanael's early life or occupation, but we do know that he and his brother Philip were searching for Christ. They were part of a group that followed John the Baptist. Jesus found Philip and Scripture tells us that Jesus's words to him were "Follow me." Philip agreed and immediately went to find his brother, Nathanael.

The Leadership Story:
Nathanael Speaks before Thinking

In John 1:46, we see Nathanael speaking before he thinks. Often when words tumble from our mouths, we reveal our raw, honest, and innermost thoughts. After Phillip comes to him, telling him that they have found Christ, Nathanael blurts out, "Nazareth! Can anything good come from there?" Words escape our lips before thinking.

This unguarded comment displayed a common perception of Nazareth. If Galilee was the end of the earth, Nazareth was the smallest and quietest town in the area. Little is known about Nazareth because it was in the middle of nowhere and nothing important ever went on there. Most people in this region were farmers with simple homes and ordinary lives. In general, people from Nazareth were considered simple, ordinary, and obscure.[3] When Nathanael made his comment about Nazareth, most people of that time would have understood and agreed that nothing could be expected from Nazareth.

But greatness does not come from size or renown. Nazareth becomes one of the most important places in history because of the overarching Glory Story of Jesus Christ. We see Nathanael speaking before thinking, before he follows Jesus and joins the community of disciples. In the company of others, especially Jesus, perhaps he gained a greater self-awareness.

Leadership Life Stories Principle:
Developing Self-awareness

Nathanael actively searches for truth and ultimately finds it within a community. As he follows Jesus, he joins a community that includes Jesus and his fellow disciples. There is some evidence that Nathanael and Philip had earlier traveled together and heard about Jesus as they followed John the Baptist. One biblical scholar writes that "the friendship of Philip and Nathanael deepened the religious life of each of them."[4] We do not know how long the two followed John the Baptist and searched for truth. In the passage from John 1, after hearing from Philip, Nathanael gets up and walks toward Jesus (1:47). As we see in Nathanael's life, developing leadership life stories is an active process that can grow when we follow Jesus within a community of believers.

As we develop our leadership life stories, time spent in a faithful community is important. It is also important to have time by ourselves and in solitude. In John 1:47–51, Nathanael has his first recorded conversation with Jesus and seems to balance both the community and time alone. The interactions between Jesus and Nathanael in these verses is an interesting back and forth. "Here truly is an Israelite in whom there is no deceit." Nathanael responds, "How do you know me?" Jesus explains, "I saw you while you were still under the fig tree before Phillip called you."

Nathanael also searches for the truth in solitude. The fig tree in this story plays an important role. In early Israel, fig trees were places for thinking, like modern day coffee shops. At Nathanael's time, these were some of the only shady spots to avoid the sun and feel the cool breeze. Sitting under a fig tree showed that Nathanael engaged moments of solitude to think and reflect. Reflection in solitude is an important part of developing self-awareness, as is the presence of strong community. The story of Nathanael and the fig tree lead us to also consider other practical aspects of creating our leadership life story of self-awareness.

Speakers and storytellers show self-awareness as they choose one theme that is developed with good structure that smoothly moves the audience from beginning, middle, to end. Using verbal and nonverbal techniques, the storyteller brings in the audience and engages them toward a greater moment of shared meaning. While there are many definitions of what a story is, this book uses the seemingly simple definition offered by Daniel Taylor in *The Healing Power of Stories*: "A story is the telling of the significant actions of characters over time."[5] This specific definition highlights four important elements of stories:

1. **Telling**. There is a power in communication interaction and there is also a give and take involved in telling and listening to a story. When I tell a story or listen to your story, we connect on another level and learn from each other.

2. **Significant action**. A story highlights a significant action. This pivotal moment is identified and then a meaning is developed. A good story will use that action to highlight a change or transformation in individuals.

3. **Characters**. The best stories focus on a person. When sharing a story, our unique insight and perspectives are shared.

4. **Time**. Most stories have a bracket or time frame that is intentionally set by the teller to create a new message or new perspective. Hopefully, our stories are new and interesting, but even in a common story, something new can be learned and then shared with others.

With this definition as our backdrop, we can now move on to the important step of figuring out the time frame and intentionally setting the brackets that frame our story. Great leadership life stories focus on one main point that is framed for the understanding of the audience; remember, our goal is to achieve shared meaning.

Leadership Life Stories Principle: Understanding the [Bracket]

The concept of leadership life stories began for me with a fortuitous encounter at a local library with Stephen Denning's book *The Springboard Story*.[6] I was excited to finally see ideas in print about the power of storytelling in personal and professional lives that were like mine. This interest continued as I read Boas Shamir's writings. Denning and most other authors and speakers suggest that a good story has a beginning, a middle, and an end. How we look at our leadership life stories depends on where we place the brackets around stories.

A *bracket* is the intentional placement or frame around an event that highlights a certain idea, and it is chosen with the individual (speaker) and the community (audience) in mind. Brackets help the speaker discern and focus on the story's theme by signifying to the listener that the story begins at this point and ends at that specific time. Where we place the brackets helps in the development of our meaning for leadership life stories. Some stories are short, and it is easy to see where the brackets are placed. Decorating the house for Christmas on a Monday night is a good example, with one event and one time frame to choose from. Some stories, however, develop over months, for example, a story about my summer job working asphalt on the road crew. Some stories may not have an ending bracket; for example, stories of relationships that are 30, 40, or 50 years or longer and that continue. The brackets we place around our leadership life stories are helpful to limit the information so that we can try to make sense of a situation.

Action Steps

Leadership life stories of self-awareness are developed in solitude and in moments of community. At their core, leadership life stories of self-awareness help individuals understand who they are and begin to develop their characteristics of leadership. My leadership life story of self-awareness about the ill-sent email helped me develop a humble attitude. The same is true with Nathanael. His leadership life story of self-awareness brought him from a solitary spot under a fig tree to a relationship with Jesus Christ. Let me encourage you to take the next steps to develop your leadership life story of self-awareness. Remember that every leadership life story has one core idea from which meaning and the main ideas flow.

1. **Step One**. What is your intentional time of day to seek solitude? If you do not have this time scheduled, let me encourage you to stop during the day, turn off the glare of social media, and rest in the shade of a fig tree.

2. **Step Two**. Sit down and spend some time looking at the pictures and notes from the earlier chapters. Using only seven words, summarize your story. For example, one of my leadership life stories is summed up as: "Listening: begins with ears, moves to heart."

At this stage of development in your leadership life story, do not get hung up on the details. If you focus on this development stage and grow around one theme, the audience has a greater chance of staying focused. As we see in Nathanael's life, shared meaning comes from times of solitude and a sense of community. Leaders who take their cues from models of shalom spend time reflecting in solitude and nurturing community. With one main focus, effective leadership life stories flow smoothly from beginning to middle to end, keeping the speaker and the audience on the same page.

Discussion Questions

1. Why do we need to limit the information in a leadership life story? What may happen if we do not?

2. Have you ever experienced an imbalance of solitude and community? Name some practical reasons why this balance is necessary.

3. What are some of the places where you find solitude? Why are these places important to you?

4. Name some places where you find energy in community. Why are these moments fulfilling for you?

Chapter 7

Thomas: Leadership
Life Stories of Struggle

Then Thomas (also known as Didymus) said to the rest of the disciples, "Let us also go, that we may die with him."

—John 11:16

Unless I see the nail marks in his hands, and put my finger where the nails were, and put my hand into his side, I will not believe.

—John 20:25

WE ARE GIVEN MORE INFORMATION ABOUT each of the second group of disciples: Nathanael, Thomas, Philip, and Matthew. Their unique characteristics and personalities emerge through the stories shared about each of them. While Thomas is typically labeled the Doubter, he can also be seen as an example of bravery, strength, and leadership in the midst of struggle. Thomas seems pessimistic and expected the worst at all times and in all situations. After the crucifixion, Thomas was so deeply burdened by what he saw and his actions in that moment that he just wanted to be alone to process the event. Though he is often called Doubting Thomas, I believe that a better picture of Thomas is one who feels emotions deeply and engages in the struggle.

Leadership life stories of struggle provide an example of working through gloomy episodes and difficult times to see the light of Jesus and his Glory Story. Leadership life stories are organized around one theme with solid structures that draw in the audience, move smoothly through the main points and build to the big idea, and then conclude with a new idea for the listener.

Calling the Disciples: Thomas

Thomas is listed eight times in Scripture. We know that he comes from Galilee, but nothing is noted in the Bible about his family, his job, or anything else about his life. Most discussions about Thomas begin with John 20:24–29.

As the other disciples return after seeing the physically risen Christ, Thomas replies, "Unless I see the nail marks in his hands and put my finger where the nails were, and put my hand into his side, I will not believe" (John 20:25). Since that moment, he has been called Doubting Thomas throughout recorded history. While this is an important passage, there are others in the Gospels that provide deeper insight into the character of Thomas.

The Leadership Story: Thomas the Realist

We hear about Thomas for the first time in John 11 in the story of the raising of Lazarus from the dead. In this passage, we see the depth of his emotions and his strong commitment to Jesus. John 11 says that Jesus was out of Jerusalem, preaching in another town across the Jordan River when news reached him that Lazarus was sick and was likely going to die. It appears that preaching in Jerusalem at the time was dangerous for Jesus and his followers. Twice in the past four months, priests had come after Jesus and tried to find ways to physically harm him.

In the Lazarus story, Jesus does not go to Mary, Martha, and Lazarus right away; instead, he waits a few days after receiving the news. I wonder if Jesus and the disciples debated going back into the potentially dangerous environment? Jesus eventually chooses to travel back to Jerusalem. The disciples immediately argue because they appear to be scared to return to Jerusalem and the danger is still there.

It is at this point that Thomas enters the story. His comment drops in verse 11: "Let us also go, that we may die with him." I appreciate the reaction of Thomas in this leadership life story of struggle. Thomas steps up in this pivotal leadership moment to encourage strength and determination from the rest of the disciples. As one theologian remarked, "He [Thomas] was a realist who saw danger clearly, yet immediately proposed the action the situation demanded."[1]

The Leadership Story: Thomas and the Need to Ponder

The second example of effective leadership communication from Thomas is after the crucifixion in John 20:24–29. Thomas has the famous line in this passage when he says, "Unless I see the nail marks in his hands, and put my finger where the nails were, and put my hand into his side, I will not believe"

(John 20:25). Often the belief of the other disciples contrasts with the doubt of Thomas, but there are several aspects we may fail to consider. What if Thomas needed time to process the overwhelming events of the crucifixion? We often forget that none of the other disciples believed until they saw Jesus either. Why do we forget the doubt of Peter and John when the women came back from the tomb? Peter, John, and many others refused to believe that Christ was alive and rushed to see the physically risen Savior. It is possible that Thomas was away from the other disciples during these first hours of the resurrection because he was still struggling with the crucifixion.

During this struggle, Thomas apparently felt a need to ponder. He took a moment—in fact, an entire week—to process the emotions and the situation. Thomas is the one disciple who shows the struggle between facts and emotions. He possessed a passionate, poetic nature, fervent in both belief and skepticism, guided more by the emotions of his heart than the logic of his mind.[2] Thomas reflected at a time of struggle, providing a framework for us as we develop a leadership life story of struggle.

Leadership Life Stories Principle:
Sharing a Good Story

Leadership life stories are effective when they show a significant action or transformation through an introduction that draws in, main points that build to a climax, and a conclusion that shares a new perspective or new idea. Writing a great story does not start at the beginning and follow a straight line. I believe we need to write our leadership life stories by messing around in the middle. Writing a great story is from the inside out.

Main Points That Build a Structure

The main points of a story are the important facts and descriptions that the speaker uses as a structure on which to build. Especially in verbal storytelling, it is most effective to keep your story to just two or three main points. It is only after we have an effective direction for our story and main points framed that we work on the introduction and conclusion.

An Introduction that Hooks

Effective stories grab the audience's attention from the first words. Starting a story with a quote, interesting statistics, or describing the sights, sounds, and smells of a moment can immediately connect with an audience and bring them into your story. I learned this lesson of effective hooks while working in radio during the thirty second weather forecast. As a local radio disc jockey, every hour I shared the upcoming weather forecast for the next day. During my monthly evaluation, my boss listened to an air-check tape and when the weather forecast came on, his eyes got heavy and he began to snore. He faked falling asleep during my feedback session, but the point was made.

My program director helped me by sharing the technique of using different descriptive words to grab attention. Instead of the usual "Expect rain this morning," use the internal thesaurus that we all have in our brains to try new words: drizzle, sprinkle, dribble, downpour, or other words. Connect well with your audience from the very beginning of the time together. Every moment with someone, even a brief one, is a moment to connect, and using interesting quotes, statistics, and description can draw the listener.

A Conclusion Providing a New Idea

Faithful communicators understand that sharing a story for a common lesson can be boring. You've taken the time to consider a seven-word approach to surface your theme for the story. You then started in the middle of story to map out the two or three main points and then hooked the audience with a creative introduction. Conclusions are the final moment to bring this whole process together and offer your lesson, with the hope that the listener will learn something new. Conclusions are the payoff; they are your opportunity to present the new idea or new perspective that your story contributes to the audience's learning.

Action Steps

It is time to begin writing your leadership life story following these steps:

1. **Step One**. List your seven-word main point of the story. Why are you talking?

2. **Step Two**. Begin in the middle and list the two or three main points you want to cover in the story. Consider: why are these important to include?

3. **Step Three**. How can you effectively grab the attention of the audience? What interesting facts, word phrases, or quotes can you use to hook the audience?

4. **Step Four**. Consider how you are going to build to the final moment of the story. How can you wrap up these thoughts to lead to a new perspective?

We see in Thomas an effective example of taking time to process one's emotions and step up into the leadership moment to inspire others. His leadership life story of struggle provides a framework for us as we move forward. It is important to realize that although we experience times of struggle, Jesus does not dismiss these low points. He invites us to come near, to question, and to believe. Jesus meets us where we are in our joys and in the gloomy places so that the light of the Glory Story shines through. As we continue with these different models of shalom, we must open our eyes and engage in the struggle as we begin to see new perspectives in our lives.

Discussion Questions

1. Do you see any of Thomas's qualities in yourself? Which ones? How can those help you be a more effective leader?

2. What is the best introduction you can recall? It might be from a sermon, a stand-up comedian's monologue, or the opening of a class. Why was it so effective?

3. Begin to think about the stories from leaders that made an impact on you. Write down why these are important to you.

4. How much time do you take to ponder or think about events, like Thomas? Why?

Chapter 8

Philip: Leadership Life Stories of New Perspective

> When Jesus looked up and saw a great crowd coming toward him, he said to Philip, "Where shall we buy bread for these people to eat?" He asked this only to test him, for he already had in mind what he was going to do.
>
> —John 6:5–6

PHILIP APPEARS TO BE THE DATA person of the organization. His narrow focus on numbers almost caused him to miss the overarching work of the Glory Story. Philip is the one who was always planning, organizing, and calculating. In John 6 and the story of feeding the 5,000, Philip is overwhelmed and beaten down, yet he comes back stronger through the strength of the Lord. Leadership life stories of new perspective describe times in our lives where a person or situation helped us see something about leadership in a new light for our personal or professional growth.

Philip is mentioned seven times in the Gospels and once in the book of Acts. Like the apostles Simon Peter and Andrew, he is from Bethsaida, a small town that is mostly known as a fishing village. In John 1:43, it is recorded that Jesus sought out and personally called Philip with the words "Follow me." Throughout the Gospels, Philip appears to have the heart of an evangelist, but sometimes he seems overwhelmed by the big picture. When thinking about leadership life stories, it is often in these times of being overwhelmed that a new perspective can emerge.

The Leadership Story of Philip: Heart of an Evangelist in the Big Picture

In John 6:5, thousands of people follow Jesus to hear him teach. In the middle of the crowds and chaos, Philip seems to be preoccupied by the details of the day. Philip is the one making plans and organizing the crowd. I imagine the shouts and excited voices of a large crowd. I can see people rushing from here to there to figure out the logistics of moving from place to place. In the middle of all this hustle, Jesus stops and asks Philip how to feed 5,000 people. I can see Philip look up at the crowd. As he looks from group to group, the tension builds in his eyes as he realizes the task in front of him. Philip is overwhelmed by the impossible. It is in this moment that Jesus shows him the possible.

Philip's strong grasp of math kept him from taking risks. His focus on the hard facts overshadowed his faith, making him blind to the spiritual possibilities that Jesus's power could offer.[1] As the story continues, a collection is taken and just five loaves of bread and two fish are found. Jesus blesses the food and the distribution begins. At the end of the story, everyone is full, everyone is satisfied, and Philip has a new perspective.

Leadership Life Stories Principle: Physical and Emotional Preparation

In looking at the life of Philip and the story of feeding the 5,000, we can see a life of readiness and faithfulness. Leadership life stories are developed out of experience. It is the best experience that exhibits physical and emotional presence. We can only be present in a valuable sense when we are physically and emotionally prepared. Two concepts that help faithful communicators as they develop leadership life stories of new perspective are the value of physical preparation and emotional preparation.

Engaging New Perspectives: Being Emotionally Prepared

Philip was emotionally ready to take up the call of leadership because of an understanding of the bigger world around him. As faithful communicators seeking to build shalom in a broken world, we should engage in a deep awareness of the world in all its depth. Details about Philip and his life show us that he was ready to engage the big picture. Grounded in his beliefs yet aware of the influence of those around him, Philip reveals how a leadership life story of new perspective can be effective.

We know that Philip was born and grew up in Bethsaida.[2] At the time of Philip's call by Jesus into the ministry, his small town's name meant "fish house." Throughout Philip's growing up years, Greek influence strengthened in the area, likely resulting in some transformations for the region. It is possible that Philip came from a home that was receptive to new ideas and had an appreciation of different cultural influences. Philip was not a Jewish but a Greek name. Based on this and the short stories we see in the scriptures, Philip may have understood his bigger calling. Jesus "welcomed a man whose name indicated an appreciation of the wider world around him."[3]

When we engage other perspectives during the development of our leadership life stories, we prepare ourselves emotionally for new ideas. We also open a wider world of possibilities in work experiences and relationships. The only way to engage these perspectives is to listen compassionately and with focus. This kind of humble focus strengthens both our leadership and our communication skills. Faithful communicators engage in tough conversations with care and focus, which provides opportunities to think and process new information and new situations.

Engaging New Perspectives: Being Physically Prepared

It appears that Philip was not one to push himself forward. Three of the four times Philip was recorded in the Gospels, Jesus comes to him. According to Smith, "In the four incidents recorded of him, three times he is sought out by others."[4] First, Philip was called by Jesus in John 1:43. Scripture says: "The next day Jesus decided to leave for Galilee. Finding Philip, he said to him, 'Follow me.'" Next, Jesus goes to Philip during the feeding of the 5,000 (John 6:5) and asks him, "Where shall we buy bread for these people?" The third time Philip is sought is found in John 12:21, where Scripture states that some Greeks came to Philip to introduce them to Jesus. In each of these moments, Philip was physically present and ready to serve.

Philip was not looking for a platform to elevate himself. He did not publicize himself or push his way into situations but when he was sought, it appears that Philip responded. He was engaged, physically present, and ready to serve. Philip is marked by his willingness to respond physically. As faithful communicators seeking to build shalom in a broken world, there is the need to be physically present and be ready to engage new people and in new situations.

Leadership Life Stories Principle: Story-Sharing Techniques

Faithful communicators share stories that focus on one theme, develop with good structure, and end with a change of perspective or twist at the end of the story. When sharing great stories, faithful communicators should consider how much information is supplied during the verbal storytelling event. It is important to provide just enough information to keep the audience's attention. A faithful communicator wants to show the audience that he is present—that he considers what his audience needs. Each audience is different. Faithful communicators need to be in tune and able to pick up on an audience's perspective. Strong verbal skill in communication connects with the audience by using some simple techniques.

1. **Connect with voice**. We all have a unique way of talking and forming words. Adjusting the pacing, pitch, and volume of your voice can add a dynamic element. Speeding up and closing the space between words can show excitement. Lowering your pitch can add seriousness to the story. For example, I was working with an organizational manager as he talked about his daughter. It was interesting to watch and hear as he switched from "office mode" to "family mode" when sharing his story. His pacing slowed down when he spoke of his family. You could see and hear the smile in his voice, and his change in tone conveyed pride in his daughter's accomplishments. A small change in the voice can make big difference as you tell your leadership life story.

2. **Connect with vivid descriptions**. Colorful language and word pictures help engage the mind of the audience and pull them into your story. If possible, engage in the five senses of sight, sound, smell, taste, and touch, to make a story come alive. As a simple exercise, consider the dog I had when I was just a baby. We called her "Killer." What picture of a dog popped into your thoughts? A big German Shepherd, a fierce Rottweiler, a solid Pit Bull? Actually, Killer was a small, black miniature Poodle named Tammy. She had the puffs of hair at the bottom of her legs and end of her tail. We called her Killer because of the cockroaches in the apartment. When the lights turned on, she chased these bugs and killed some of them before they escaped. Providing good details and just enough description can help an audience track with your story.

3. **Connect with dialogue**. Many of our stories contain characters. Using their voices and their words paints a picture in the mind of the audience. Using different tones or accents brings the characters to life. Dialogue can add an element of humor, drama, and depth to your story. Closely tied to dialogue, using the same word to start a new thought or using the distinct and unique way your characters speak can add interest and variety to your story.

With these thoughts in mind, let me offer one of my leadership life stories of new perspectives. While this is my written transcript of the story, when I share this story in person, I verbally use some of the suggestions above.

Have you ever had one of those moments that took your breath away? In our leadership life stories of new perspective, I have been thinking about those moments where we can breathe again, which enables us to keep taking positive steps forward. As a kid, my brothers and I would ride our bikes down to a drainage ditch a few blocks away. We would tear along this knee-high culvert, pedaling with all of our might to launch ourselves when the drain made a left-hand turn. Often you could grab some pretty good air and land with a thud and a yell of triumph. Until one day, the handlebars snapped off.

The scene rolls through my mind in slow motion. I was ripping down the chute on my yellow Schwinn bike with a matching yellow banana seat. When I came to the bend, I pulled up on the handlebars. They came off in my hands. The bike slammed into the concrete side and flipped me onto the dirt and grass, sending me end over end. I remember lying there, curled around the useless handlebars of the bike as I struggled for breath. On the ground, gasping for air, I am sure I looked like a just-landed fish on dry ground, my mouth opening and closing as I heard only the wheeze, deep in my lungs.

In our lives and leadership, I think we get stuck in that moment. Maybe it is our tendency to see the glass half empty or simply the emotional impact of that crushing, unexpected moment. But what about the moment immediately after? Why is it that we cannot remember that gulp of air, the sweet taste and fullness in our chest as we breathe again? At the moment I am writing this, I am walking through a life situation I hoped to never confront; I am taking steps I never wanted to take. Even just the last few days, I am confronting surreal conditions. This past week, I stepped into a picture that seemingly confirmed evidence, and gut instincts developed the past few years. I am gasping for air after a tough moment of life and leadership that takes my breath away. However, even in this difficult moment, thanks to an interaction with a friend named David, I'm gulping the sweet taste of life lived well with others.

I connected with David a few years ago. Like most dads, we had surface conversations while waiting in line to get the kids from elementary school. He knows a bit about why I'm gasping for air. David helped me take a breath of fresh air through an extended text conversation. David shared the story of his escape from his country, fearing for his life, when he was just nine years old. He floated on a fishing boat for five days and four nights with his two sisters until he was rescued. After two years of survival in a refugee camp, he was given permission to come to this community to live. Through the back and forth of text messages, I was given an opportunity to breathe with his story. David provided an example of someone who went through a terrible family event and is still breathing. His examples focused on trust in God and service to his family. He reminded me that ultimately God has everything in his hand, and I needed to be obedient. Through David's story, I was able to keep breathing. David's vulnerable story as a refugee helped me gain a new perspective so that I could take the next steps forward.

Action Steps

As we continue to work through our leadership life stories, remember one of the landmarks from Chapter 1—personal growth through solitude and community. Leaders grow and engage their personal identity in thoughts and action by themselves, but they also grow as they engage the community. Others help us test and refine personal development. This chapter's action steps involve both solitude and community.

1. **Step One**. Take some time to write down your story. Start with a blank sheet of paper or a blank computer screen. Let your fingers fly and just engage one of your leadership life stories. I have found that writing ten minutes of words is a positive first start. Do not critique the words on the page or screen. The attempt here is to engage the five senses and get the story out.

2. **Step Two**. After you have written for about ten minutes, begin to sort through the story. Engage the internal thesaurus of your life and consider the different words or phrases that you can use to highlight the five senses and connect with your audience.

3. **Step Three**. Now that you have these initial thoughts down, it is time to engage your community. Reach out to friends and family and schedule a time to begin telling this rough story. At this stage, you are not looking for perfection; instead, you are looking to vividly verbalize your pictures and thoughts.

Discussion Questions

1. Can you think of a situation that left you feeling like you could barely fill your lungs with air? What helped you overcome the challenges in this situation?

2. How can sharing one's story of a breath of fresh air help to build shalom?

3. What are your main takeaways from the writing session? Have a discussion with your friends as these thoughts continue to develop. What was easy for you in the writing session (e.g., getting started, organizing the ideas)? What was difficult for you in the writing session (e.g., staying focused, figuring out what to say)?

Chapter 9

Matthew: Leadership Life Stories of New Beginnings

He [Jesus] saw a man named Matthew sitting at the tax collector's booth. "Follow me," he told him, and Matthew got up and followed him. While Jesus was having dinner at Matthew's house, many tax collectors and sinners came and ate with him and his disciples.

—Matthew 9:9–10

THE CALL OF MATTHEW IS ONE of the most dramatic stories of redemption. It is depicted in three of the four Gospels. Right after accepting the call from Jesus, Matthew extends an invitation to his house for a celebration and encourages others to accept the free gift of salvation. Matthew does not sit around and contemplate this newly received gift—he immediately takes action to share it. Leadership life stories of new beginnings tell of a time where the leader made a mistake, learned from the challenge, and began a new action and behavior. We see this dramatically in the behavior of Matthew and the feast at his house after Jesus calls him to a new start. Matthew took immediate steps to open up a sacred space where he could share the Glory Story. This process can create a sacred space between individuals when they listen to and share stories that ultimately point back to the Glory Story of Jesus.

Calling the Disciples: Matthew

Matthew is mentioned seven times in the Bible and scholars believe that he wrote the entire book of Matthew, focusing on Jesus. He is mentioned as Levi several times in the Bible (Mark 3:18 and Luke 6:15). When we first meet Matthew, he is hated and despised by everyone because he was the tax collector for the Roman government. As a tax collector, or publican, Matthew had essentially given up his place in the community to make money. Tax collectors, or publicans, were known for their dishonesty, and having the Jewish name Levi only intensified the perception that he was betraying Israel for Rome.[1]

Tax collecting was one of the most hated occupations at this time. Matthew was part of the Jewish community, but he intentionally collected taxes from his neighbors and passed the funds along to the Roman government. By stepping into his role as a tax collector, Matthew probably alienated himself from his Jewish friends' homes.[2] He was hated by the Jewish community and considered a sinner because it was assumed tax collectors took extra money that ended up in their own pockets. He was even hated by the Romans who saw him as a traitor to his own community.[3] If the disciples were outcasts, Matthew was thought to be even lower than others because he was an outcast from both his own community and from the Romans.

Yet, Jesus accepted Matthew and his leadership life story became a testament to the Glory Story. It is interesting to consider that, as a tax collector employed by the Roman government, Matthew had to have good observation skills. He also needed to be able to keep good records. These skills were probably developed and nurtured through his work. Through his record-keeping and collecting, he probably got to know his neighbors rather well. As a tax collector, Matthew lived in Capernaum and probably knew of Jesus and the other disciples.[4] You can get to know someone well when you know their financial situation. Apparently, Matthew welcomed many that he knew after he was called by Jesus. Considering Matthew's position, some of those he welcomed may not have been part of the socially accepted crowd. But Matthew built bridges to those around him, sharing the news of what Jesus Christ had done for him.

The Leadership Story: New Beginnings for All

As Matthew invites others to accept the free gift of salvation at a banquet at his home, it is interesting to note how he goes from taking to giving. He definitely has enemy status as he takes tax money for the government—then Jesus enters his life. Then he becomes a friend to all, giving away the free gift of salvation through Jesus Christ. Through Matthew's leadership life story of new beginnings, we have a model of shalom that shows the importance of dying to the old life and resurrecting the new life that Jesus Christ made possible for us.

Matthew's leadership life story speaks to us on several levels. In all three of the passages where the story is found (see Matt. 9:9–13, Mark 2:13–17, and Luke 5:27–32), Matthew throws a large banquet and invites others just like him to the feast. Practically, he creates a sacred space for those he invites, opening the possibility of spiritual rebirth for his guests. Spiritually, he opens a sacred space for any who wish to meet and accept Jesus. Scripture notes that the teachers of law criticized Jesus and Matthew for the sinners who ate at the table. Jesus reminds the spiritual elite of the time that his Glory Story goes out to everyone.

Matthew abandoned the pleasures and temptations of the world for the promise of eternal life and then he moved immediately to share that promise with others. Matthew's leadership life story shows how one who is flawed and trapped in sin can walk away from that life to follow Jesus. His new beginning changes his own life but also impacts those around him that he welcomes so graciously. Faithful communicators seeking a model of shalom can find one in Matthew, whose practical and spiritual actions created a sacred space for others.

Leadership Life Stories Principle: From Before to After

Leadership life stories of new beginnings are stories that describe the before and the after of a leadership situation. These leadership life stories are all around us. As people of faith, some examples of leadership life stories are those in our faith communities who changed their view and changed their lives because of a testimony.

I work at an institution that does not expressly profess faith. I am grateful for the continued work of the Holy Spirit and how people are stirred to make a commitment for a life with Jesus Christ. One of these people, we will call her Sarah, was a student in my first-year classes. When I connected with her, she was a new freshman student trying to figure out school and life while being away from home for the first time. During the time in this first academic year, Sarah got connected to a Bible study on campus. Through a mentoring relationship with the leaders in the group, she made a commitment to Jesus Christ as her Lord and Savior.

Sarah's final persuasive speech of the semester was a joy for me. I remember the weeks leading up to the speech. Through an email she asked if she could share her testimony, even though the speech was to be, technically, an academic topic. After I agreed, she worked through the facts, wrote out the information, and presented a speech late in the semester. Her invitation to the saving grace of Jesus Christ ended her speech. In the years since this opportunity, Sarah has shared her testimony several times and continues to reach out and invite others to accept the free gift of salvation. Both Sarah in the modern day and Matthew as a disciple experienced the new beginnings found in a personal relationship with Jesus Christ. Our leadership life stories of new beginning have the opportunity for us to be disciples and to point others to the perfect shalom found in heaven.

I would like to suggest three ideas for communities or individuals who engage leadership life stories to develop meaning in difficult times and create a new beginning.

1. **Leadership life stories are most effective when they hinge on an overarching story of meaning**. For me, that overarching story comes from my faith. My personal leadership life story has been developed through my personal relationship with the Lord. It is through this unchanging truth that I can find meaning in the confusing times of destruction. This faith relationship helps me focus on a primary value as I interact with personal and physical challenges.

2. **Leadership life stories are most effective when they provide vision**. In the story of Matthew, I love how Jesus provided a simple vision with two words: "Follow me." When leadership life stories focus on the steps forward, a vision is provided so that everyone can use their unique talents and abilities. Jesus simply asks Matthew to follow him. Scripture tells us that Matthew immediately started sharing the good news to those in his circle of influence.

3. **Leadership life stories are most effective when they provide space in our thinking and in our actions**. Leadership life stories are a shift in thinking to take the time and create the space for communities and individuals to sort through the process, to build or rebuild meaning. We see these steps from different people in the Matthew story. Matthew takes a different action in Matthew 9:10 by reaching out to everyone and interacting with different ideas of his community. Scripture says that during the dinner at Matthew's house, "many tax collectors and sinners came and ate with him and his disciples" (Matt. 9:10). The religious leaders provide a different view. Instead of providing a space to engage different perspectives, Scripture says in verse 11: "When the Pharisees saw this, they asked his disciples, 'Why does your teacher eat with tax collectors and sinners?'" Leadership life stories open the mind and the heart to seek understanding through our actions. Matthew provides a wonderful example of how faithful communicators can engage their communities.

Great Stories through Nonverbal Communication

Presenting a great story involves not only content and verbal expression, but it requires nonverbal skill as well. When a speaker offers something new to those listening through the verbal and also shows involvement non-verbally, communication is strengthened. When you allow your body to get in on the action, you show commitment to your audience and to your story. Leaders like Matthew who present great stories can reach others on a physical and spiritual level. Nonverbal communication involves physical involvement on the part of the speaker, and it often reaches emotions that the verbal alone cannot. Here are some tips for nonverbal communication that can strengthen your leadership life story.

1. **Eye Contact**. Eye contact is a wonderful way to engage listeners. It is often said that the eyes are the window to the soul. By making eye contact with individuals when sharing your story, you may have the ability to comprehend their understanding. It is important to remember that people are looking into your eyes as well. When we soften our gaze and invite eye contact, we can better connect and genuinely engage those around us.

2. **Facial Expressions**. In addition to the eyes, your face can be an effective tool to convey emotions and connect with the audience. We all have facial expressions that should match the mood of our leadership life story. Smiling, frowning, the raise of an eyebrow, or widening your eyes can all help emphasize different aspects of the plot and characters in your story.

3. **Gestures and Body Movement**. Using hand gestures helps the audience track and follow your leadership life story. These gestures can illustrate actions, describe objects, or emphasize certain points in the story. Gestures make the story more dynamic and visually exciting. Leaning in or taking a step back from the audience can also add interest and strengthen emotional connection with the audience.

Action Steps

As we wrap up this second section of the book, consider the development of your leadership life stories. Consider how far we have come since the opening of this book. The steps below can help you revisit and gather some wisdom from our earlier discussions and prepare you for our future steps.

1. **Step One**. Take a moment to review what you have individually written down in your notes from the previous chapter. Hopefully, you will connect with some people in your community and have shared your leadership life stories with them. Assess how that felt. What adjustments do you need to make in the writing of your leadership life story? Are more facts or descriptive phrases needed?

2. **Step Two**. Remember to enjoy the process. The feedback from our community, both encouraging and challenging, is helping us grow in our faith and in our leadership life stories. Listen well and think critically and constructively about the feedback you are receiving. Be open to using nonverbal techniques to emphasize your vision and to point to the overarching story of meaning.

We are over halfway through this process of thinking about and writing down our leadership life story, so let's look at where we have been. We took the step in Section One as agents of Shalom to discover some of the possible topics and areas of leadership in your life. Section Two offered four types of leadership life stories as models of shalom to help develop an effective script that focused on one overarching theme. This theme moved smoothly from point to point to point and prepared you to write the leadership life story with creative words and engaging nonverbal communication. The final section will offer four examples from the disciples who seem to be closest to Jesus. These witnesses to shalom are first-century leaders who encourage twenty-first century leaders to reflect the Glory Story of Jesus Christ through some of their values.

Discussion Questions

1. Have you ever seen someone move from unbelief to belief or from a despised position in community to a favored one? Or have you heard such a story told? What made it striking?

2. How would you define a sacred space? What makes this place important to you? How can your leadership life story lead to one?

3. As a leader, how can you help create a sacred space for others?

Section Three

WITNESSES TO SHALOM

Chapter 10

James the Greater: Son of Thunder

When the disciples James and John saw this, they asked, "Lord, do you want us to call fire down from heaven to destroy them?" But Jesus turned and rebuked them.

—Luke 9:54–55

THERE IS A PLACE FOR FAITHFUL communicators who have booming personalities—people like James the Greater. James is half of the Sons of Thunder, brother to the Apostle John. James the Greater has a fiery temperament and a brash personality. He often speaks before thinking. As a witness to shalom, James the Greater provides an example of the importance of living and learning in community.

This third section of the book offers examples from the last group of the disciples who follow Jesus. This group of disciples—James, Andrew, John, and Peter—appear to be the closest to Jesus during his ministry and we have more information about each of them. As witnesses to the Glory Story of Jesus Christ, these disciples demonstrate through their words and behavior how we can act as faithful communicators. Let's consider some first-century leaders who can provide examples to us in the twenty-first century.

Calling the Disciples: James the Greater

James the Greater is one of Jesus's inner circle among the disciples. The several times he is mentioned in the Bible, he appears to be in a group of people that is closest to Jesus. In this group we do know much more about the disciples. In Matthew 4:18–20 and in Mark 1:16–20, John and James are in a fishing community. When Jesus calls them to ministry, the brothers immediately drop their nets and follow Jesus. James the Greater appears to engage by living and learning in a community. Intense feelings and a big personality are characteristics of James the Greater. The two times James's words are recorded in the Gospels (Luke 9:53 and Mark 10:35–40), he appears to be impatient, outspoken, and intense toward evildoers. Jesus used the Greek word *boanerges* to remind James and John when they let their naturally feverish temperaments get out of hand. *Boanerges* appropriately "defines James' personality in very vivid terms. He was zealous, thunderous, passionate, and fervent."[1] Throughout the three years of ministry, Jesus appears to provide space so that James can make mistakes and then learn from these mistakes.

The Leadership Story: Correction in Community

The leadership life story of James the Greater in Luke 9:51–56 reinforces the value of correction within an emotionally healthy community. A bit of background is needed to understand the situation depicted in this story. Jesus, near the end of his earthly ministry, was getting ready to return to Jerusalem. To get to the city, he must walk through a Samaritan village. There was deep-seated animosity between the Jewish and Samaritan people, so the scene was set for significant tension. It appears that James and John wanted to go directly to Jerusalem instead of adding miles to the trip by going around the village. Messengers were sent to the Samaritan village to try and find a place to rest, only to discover that all of the doors were closed to those headed to Jerusalem. They returned with a negative report that Jesus and his disciples were not welcome into the Samaritan territory.

James and John are angry. Armed with their seemingly justified righteous anger, they seek worldly revenge. "Lord, do you want us to call fire down from heaven to destroy them?" they ask in Luke 9:54. You can see and hear the emotional intensity of the moment. Jesus stops them immediately. Luke 9:55 says, "Jesus turned and rebuked them." Jesus knew the strong personality of James, referring to him earlier as a Son of Thunder. While we do not know the exact words Jesus used in the rebuke, I'm sure they were strong, direct, and clear.

Let's focus, however, on the nonverbal reply of Jesus in verse 56. Scripture simply says, "Then he [Jesus] and his disciples went to another village." Consider the impact that Jesus's nonverbal communication may have had on James. By not arguing and causing a scene, Jesus helps James understand an important step in being a witness to shalom. As faithful communicators, even those with big personalities can realize that a small behavior can be powerful. As a witness to shalom, "Jesus's example taught James that loving-kindness and mercy are virtues to be cultivated as much as righteous indignation and fiery zeal."[2] This is all we hear from Scripture of this story.

I assume that James learned from Jesus how to take correction and when to use his thunderous personality. The emotionally healthy community of Jesus and the disciples allowed space to express emotions, to receive correction as James did, and to move forward in shalom.

Leadership Life Stories Principle:
Power within Community

I had long wanted to visit the "Pompeii of the North" in Iceland—located just a few miles off the southern coast and within the Westman Islands. During the summer of 2019, I finally had the opportunity to visit. The story of this place speaks not only of catastrophe and resilience but reflects the power of community in leadership life stories. In 1973, a mile-wide gash ripped open the earth in the town of Heimaey just off the southern coast of Iceland. The volcano erupted on the evening of January 23, and the community of about 5,000 people were quickly evacuated to the mainland while crawling lava threatened the fishing harbor and the heart of the community. As the volcano Eldfell emerged, the belching magma and floating ash permanently changed the landscape of the island and the lives among the Vestmannaeyjar Islands.[3]

I'm especially drawn to the creative solution used to protect the harbor and the community. The lava threatened to choke the harbor and cut off the fishing production plants. They implemented a plan to spray seawater on the advancing flow to cool the lava, stop the advance, and form and extend the harbor. Not only was their main industry of fishing protected, but the quick initial action and intentional planning over the five months of the eruption also helped the town bounce back. Hiking to the top of the volcano almost fifty years after the eruption and still feeling the warm touch of the rock on top of Eldfell, I found myself thinking about resilience formed in a community.

While on the summit, I talked to a German couple who last visited the island in 1979, just a few years after the town and island began their recovery. They were amazed at the difference in the community and impressed by how the town had made a comeback since the eruption. Considering all that Jesus and the disciples faced in those three years of ministry, it is clear that James specifically and the community of disciples generally also showed resilience as individuals and as a community.

I appreciate the review of the term resilience and the several definitions of the term in a U.S. Department of Energy report. The specific aspect of resilience that I'm going to use centers on the initial shock or adversity and the ability to bounce back with positive adaptations.[4] It is interesting to consider that the initial shock or adversity that moves one to resilience can be a negative event, but it can also have positive results.

It is easy for me to see personal examples of resilience. My children are getting to the age where they are out of the house more often. They are usually with friends, at work, or doing things at school and in the community. This entails positive shocks and adversity. In newfound freedom we encounter difficult situations that we often learn from. I pray that my children continue to appropriately enjoy their freedom as they grow into adults. One of the adaptations I have made to their new freedom is to continue to be involved and active in their lives. For example, I often join them in some of their sports and theatre activities. I have seen other parents implement activities that create positive results as well. A friend detailed on Facebook that since her daughter is now out of the house working her part-time job most evenings, they intentionally get together for their family time during the lunch hour. Rather than focusing on the negative effects of a change, this family has shown resilience by nurturing new positive opportunities to connect.

The town of Heimaey has experienced several positive communal results from their shock and adversity. At the time of the eruption, many residents who were evacuated were given housing in the other Icelandic towns and cities. My colleagues in the northern city of Akureyri said that during Heimaey's recovery, several Vestmannaeyjahusin (Westman Island houses) were built for those evacuated from the island. Once the eruption stopped, people moved back to the island and slowly began to rebuild. Water lines were dug under the hot lava to provide natural energy and heat to this far north town. For the next fifty years, the Northern cod fishing in this town rose to global importance. The time I spent on Vestmannaeyjar helped me focus on the idea of resilience in a new way.

Witnesses to Shalom: Learning in an Emotionally Healthy Community

The story of James the Greater reveals how leaders can build their leadership life stories by bringing a glimpse of shalom into a broken world. The impact of an emotionally healthy community is clearly seen in this interaction between James, his brother, and Jesus. When we interact in an emotionally healthy fashion with our community, we lead by example. Mistaken reactions are dealt with wisely, change is made, and a positive outcome is evident to all. When we act as witnesses to shalom, we acknowledge that we live in a broken world that yearns for the perfect goodness and harmony of heaven. Shalom provides opportunities for heaven to cut through the arguments and chaos of our broken world and point back to the perfect interaction between the Father, Jesus the Son, and the Holy Spirit. As we conclude this chapter, let me offer a couple action steps to help leaders with big personalities live and learn in a healthy community.

Action Steps

1. **Step One**. Use your big personality for a big purpose. In what communities are you currently involved? List four or five groups that you actively participate in each month. For example, I interact with my faith community on Sundays and we also get together during the week. In addition, I have my work community and my family. List the different communities in which you engage.

2. **Step Two**. Consider your learning. What have you learned through the stories of the people around you with big personalities. This is where listening is an important activity to cultivate. List two values that you see in your community that you would like to build into your own life.

There is a place for faithful communicators to engage large personalities and booming voices. How these are formed in community plays an important part in sharing the Glory Story of Jesus Christ. While big personalities often take center stage, there is also a place in leadership life stories for those who are quiet and reserved; an emotionally healthy community recognizes the part that all can play. The process and practice of leadership life stories allows space for everyone seeking to make a difference in the lives of others.

Discussion Questions

1. Have you ever experienced a situation in which a small nonverbal behavior made a big difference?

2. Do you think someone can be a leader if they are quiet and reserved? Why or why not?

3. What are some of the benefits of being a big personality in leadership? What are some of the cautions?

4. As a leader, how do you temper and adjust your personality to the group that you are working with?

Chapter 11

Andrew: Listening for Truth

> Andrew, Simon Peter's brother, was one of the two who heard
> what John had said and who had followed Jesus. The first thing
> Andrew did was to find his brother Simon and tell him, "We
> have found the Messiah" (that is, the Christ). And he brought
> him to Jesus.
>
> —John 1:40–42

THERE IS A PLACE IN SPIRITUAL leadership for those with quiet personalities. Andrew is one of the core group of disciples that seems to be the
closest to Jesus. He is always listed in the core group of the disciples with
Peter, James, and John. While Andrew searched for truth through a personal relationship with Jesus Christ, he was willing to serve others behind
the scenes rather than be front and center. There are times that Andrew is
left out of common experiences, like the healing of Jarius's daughter or the
Garden of Gethsemane. Yet, Andrew still served Jesus well even though he
was not center stage. Andrew had "the grace to accept being left out."[1]

I like to imagine that Andrew may have been an introvert and enjoyed
spending time in silence and with his own thoughts. But he was a people
person as well—one who seemed to value friendships. As a witness to shalom, Andrew searched for a deep, personal connection with others to better
understand himself and those around him.

Andrew was willing to subject himself to sacrifice and hardship in
pursuit of truth. Andrew is seen 12 times in the Bible. Most of the time
he is mentioned as the brother of Simon in the Gospels, never the other
way around. In the early history of the church, Andrew is recognized as
an apostle primarily known as Simon Peter's brother.[2] As one of the final
group of disciples that is most intimate with Jesus, it is surprising that he is
so quiet. Andrew seemed to know his gifts and role in the ministry of Jesus
Christ. As someone who is often in community with others, matched with a
quiet personality, Andrew may have had insight that other disciples missed.

Calling the Disciples: Andrew

Since Andrew was a fisherman, we can assume that he was strong and able to handle great challenges in the water and on land. Some commentators write that Andrew's name can be translated as "manly."[3] The first disciple Jesus calls to ministry is Andrew. His quick response reveals that he thirsted for truth and found it in an eternal relationship with Jesus Christ. We know that Andrew was in search of truth. One of the first mentions of Andrew in the book of John, Chapter 1 says "Andrew, Simon Peter's brother, was one of the two who heard what John had said and who had followed Jesus" (v. 40). This verse identifies Andrew as part of the community following John the Baptist, the wandering prophet who traveled through Israel and proclaimed the coming Messiah. It is not clear how long Andrew followed John the Baptist, but his quest for truth led him through the difficult and challenging landscape of early Israel. One day while John the Baptist preached, Jesus walked by. John the Baptist exclaimed, "Look, there goes the Lamb of God." Andrew and several others followed and listened to Jesus for several hours. After listening to Jesus for some time, Andrew found his brother Simon Peter and told him, "We have found the Messiah" (that is, the Christ). And he brought him to Jesus" (vv. 41–42). Scripture tells us that he brought Simon Peter to Jesus.

Even though Andrew probably knew that his brother Peter would overshadow him, Andrew still brought Peter to Jesus. Andrew's actions reveal a lot about his character. Even if he was quiet and reserved, he acted immediately in the face of truth. Andrew's first priority was to introduce those he knew to Jesus Christ.

The Leadership Story: Faith in the Small Things

Even though Andrew was possibly an introvert and a quiet disciple, he knew the value of small things. Andrew developed connections as he built bridges to others. These small interactions increased his faith as he saw small things yield big results. John 6:8–13 tells the story of the feeding of the 5,000, where Andrew brings meager gifts to the Lord for his multiplication. After Philip questions how the disciples will feed so many, Andrew speaks up. He brings what seems a small thing to Jesus, saying, "Here is a boy with five small barley loaves and two small fish" (John 6:9). I can see Andrew standing with this small boy, and I can imagine the murmur of thousands of people behind him. Andrew simply presents these to the Lord, trusting that Jesus can use whatever gifts he has brought for his honor and glory. Scripture reveals Andrew as one who brings people and gifts to Jesus regardless of their seeming importance, for he knows that little is much in the Lord's hands.

Leadership Life Stories Principle: Small Gifts, Big Results

When we act as witnesses to shalom, Jesus uses our small gifts and introverted personalities for a big result. Leadership life stories have space for all because the small, quiet stories of faith can be used by the Lord. A favorite book on my shelf titled *Leadership Is an Art* by Max De Pree provides just such an example. Shadowed by other weighty scholarly works, this small book has a big lesson for those of us who think about and practice leadership.

De Pree is best known for his books *Leadership Jazz* and, my personal favorite, *Leadership Is an Art*. Not only was he a terrific writer, but he practiced great leadership as CEO of office furniture manufacturer Herman Miller. He served in different capacities with this company in west Michigan for over forty years. Additionally, his work included time with the De Pree Center for Leadership at Fuller Theological Seminary in Holland, Michigan. I did not know Max De Pree personally. I do know that his work and writing have shaped my journey in three significant ways.

First, leadership is an act of cultivating people. I have learned that leadership is not just a scientific fact to uncover. DePree states that "the measure of leadership is not the quality of the head, but the tone of the body. The signs of outstanding leadership appear primarily among the followers."[4] His books have helped me see that leadership is not just an individual endeavor or a journey into case studies where one emerges as a leader. Leadership is meant to be cultivated and encouraged among people.

Second, leadership can be shared through storytelling. I first skimmed my copy of *Leadership Is an Art* during my return to formal education. At the time, I was stumbling around a Master's degree program trying to find an academic topic. In addition to this, I was working as a human resource developer with state government, trying to figure out how to effectively foster learning in the training environment. The chapter titled "Tribal Storytelling" in *Leadership Is an Art* sketched out De Pree's understanding of sharing leadership through stories. In fact, both of De Pree's books mentioned above gently share his perspective and practice of leadership through stories. Through the stories in his books, we learn about De Pree's identity as a leader, and we also learn about organizational and community stories and their impact. His books helped me see that leadership storytelling and this concept of leadership life stories are valuable practices.

Third, leadership is a balance of process and practice. Think about the titles of the two books mentioned, *Leadership Is an Art* and *Leadership Jazz*. Art and jazz may both seem intuitive and fluid, and some may consider them unstructured. In De Pree's books, however, he presents leadership as a process that is artistic and jazz-like, but he also notes that leadership relies on the practice of good structure and efficiency. Framework is important just as much as process. De Pree's books helped me understand the importance of these, but it also taught me that leadership is not always bound by a time frame, structure, or learning event.

Spending time in community and cultivating others seems like a small thing that doesn't often merit mention on the world stage. Sharing a story seems personal, and some would consider it a small gift. The process of leadership is the daily grind, the mundane, everyday task of getting the job done. Authentic leadership doesn't fill books with diagrams, charts, statistics, and theories that define its practice. These are small gifts, but when practiced well by the faithful communicator they yield big gifts that foster shalom in a broken world.

Witnesses to Shalom: The Power of Listening Well

Listening takes courage. To listen, one has to voluntarily enter the space of another person who is created in the image of God. Often, we think about speaking as being the point of influence. I would like to offer through the example of Andrew that listening well can change the direction of someone's life. Our earlier discussion about Thaddeus (Chapter 3) centered on our action step of listening well to others and engaging this transformative power. As our leadership life stories develop, we should also acknowledge that there are times when power is evident when we are listened to. Listening well to others is an important part of the leadership process. As I reflect back on some of the more important times of my life, I'm struck by the idea that leadership also happened when a person listened to me and allowed me space to speak and formulate my thoughts while they listened.

During my undergraduate degree I was ready to drop out of college for the second time. I was struggling through the theories and class work and felt like maybe I was not college material. The situation was so bad that I called a friend in Anchorage, Alaska, began packing the car, and was ready to head north. I had a paper due for a class in the next few days. As a last attempt, I called up the professor for a meeting to get some feedback on the draft.

Standing outside his office, I was pretty intimidated—a simple, second year student struggling through the material. The professor was well known in the field with a couple of books published and speaking engagements across the country. Peeking in the office, he was typing away at the computer. I knocked on the door and immediately he stopped, turned around to face me, and used my name to invite me into his office. He moved his chair in front of mine with his back to the computer and started asking questions and listening to my replies.

Just a few minutes into our conversation, the phone behind him started to ring. The phone rang and rang and rang while the professor continued to ask questions and listen to my answers. Finally, after more than 20 rings, I told him, "Listen, feel free to get your phone." He stopped, tilted his head and it was like he finally heard what was going on in the background. He had been so focused on our back and forth that he seemed not to hear the phone ringing.

His response was the moment of listening that changed my leadership life story. He said, "Listen, that could be the President of the United States. I'm talking to you and they can call back. I'm getting the feeling, though, that this conversation is not about the paper." He moved my paper to the side of the desk. "What is really going on?" This question allowed me the opportunity to share some of my doubts about being a college student. I even shared that I was ready to move to Alaska and drop out. After a few minutes, we agreed that a move to Alaska was a bit dramatic. While the paper was not perfect, there were some good starting thoughts that could be developed. After the meeting, I unloaded the car and took the next step forward as a college student.

This moment of listening lasted less than 15 minutes, yet it changed the rest of my leadership life story and still plays an important role in my life today. There is a power when we listen to others. Not only can we listen to others as they share their stories, but listening itself can be a moment when we learn something that adds to our own leadership life story. As a witness to shalom, Andrew provides an example of effective listening and offering our small gifts to be used for God's plan.

Action Steps

Thankfully, genuine listening has a simple first step: be quiet. As we conclude this chapter about Andrew, remember that there is a place in leadership life stories for quiet personalities that seek connection. This happens when we listen well. In the previous chapters, I have asked you to engage your community and share your leadership life stories. It is now time to step up and engage the practice of good listening. During your next opportunity with someone in your family, community, or organization, take the following steps:

1. **Step One**. Engage the person sitting in front of you by orienting yourself in their direction and making good eye contact.

2. **Step Two**. Limit your distraction and remove computers and cell phones. Shut down your social media and any other noise around you.

3. **Step Three**. Stop your brain and be present and in the moment with this other person. To me, this is the most important step. With your body, mind, and heart, listen well to the person in front of you, really hearing what they are seeking to express.

Leadership life stories have room for all personalities, big and small. We are all "fearfully and wonderfully made," according to Psalm 139—both leaders and listeners. God uses introverts and extroverts to serve as witnesses to shalom in a broken world. No matter what our personalities, when we shut everything else out and focus on listening to the one God has placed in front of us, shalom breaks through.

Discussion Questions

1. When was the last time you sat with someone and focused solely on what they were expressing? What was the result?

2. Why is listening to someone difficult for you? What do you need in your mind, body, and attitude to listen well?

3. Do you see how leadership can be both *practice* (structure and efficiency) and *process* (intuitive and fluid)? Which do you lean toward, practice or process? And what do you think the value of the other is?

Chapter 12

John: Cultivated through Time

When he had gone a little farther, he saw James son of Zebedee and his brother John in a boat, preparing their nets. Without delay he called them, and they left their father Zebedee in the boat with the hired men and followed him.

—Mark 1:19–20

IN THE LIFE OF JOHN, WE see that leadership life stories begin with a moment and the learning continues over a lifetime. The beloved disciple John was the longest-serving disciple of Jesus Christ. When John was called to be a disciple, he was most likely in his late teens.[1] John provides a witness to shalom that helps us understand that leadership life stories are learned through time by making a commitment to Jesus Christ in a covenant relationship.

Calling the Disciples: John

I appreciate the call of each disciple found in the Gospels. Each call is distinct and provides insight into the unique personalities that Jesus saw in them as his ministry began. In general, Simon (Peter), Andrew, James, and John are considered the disciples closest to Jesus. Of this group, John is often called the "beloved" or referred to as "the disciple whom Jesus loved"[2]

When John was called, we see a theme develop that is repeated in the calls of several other disciples: John immediately stopped what he was doing and followed Jesus. In Mark 1:19, the four disciples who became part of the inner core were working on the fishing nets. I imagine these four talking with each other as they fixed their nets or were on the water fishing. The topic in these conversations could range from simple jokes to the big issues and concerns of life. In the little bit of fishing that I have done, there are times of self-reflection and times of listening to and sharing ideas about the deep questions of life. When

Jesus found these four on the shores, I imagine that they had already talked about their deep yearning for a savior.

There is another interesting small detail that might be overlooked in the case of John. In Mark 1:20, the writer comments that John and James "left their father Zebedee in the boat." To the families who made their lives along the Sea of Galilee, the fact that John left his father Zebedee for his father in heaven was an important statement. These two aspects of John's call play an important role in his long life, helping us to understand the deep love and deep commitment that John had as a witness to shalom. His leadership prompts us to inspect our hearts as we engage others in our leadership life stories.

The Leadership Story: Growth in Christ

John shares the name Sons of Thunder with his older brother James. As one observer shared, "Undisciplined as was this Son of Thunder, he nonetheless possessed vigorous emotional drive, deep feeling, and a passionate impulse to action."[3] Yet, over time John went from a Son of Thunder to the beloved disciple through the love of Jesus Christ. John is probably one of the closest confidants of Jesus during his ministry. He is found at the foot of the cross as Jesus is crucified, standing with Jesus's mother, Mary. Jesus looks down from the cross and tells John to protect his mother (John 19:26–27). John does this and becomes a pillar of the early church. John is exiled to the Isle of Patmos and is the only disciple who dies of old age. Even with his exile, he continued to proclaim Jesus Christ. Scottish theologian A. B. Bruce remarks, "the zeal of the son of thunder did not disappear from John's nature after he became an apostle; it only became tempered by the light of wisdom, and softened by the heat of love."[4]

Leadership Life Stories Principle: Beauty in the Ugly

During my time in Athens, Greece, in May 2023, I often heard the idea that you can find beauty in the ugly. Time after time, as I heard this phrase and thought about the connection to leadership life stories, I asked, "How?" My intent here is to offer a few thoughts on the seeming contrast between beauty and ugliness through leadership life stories that come directly from my time, and journal writing, while in Greece. After a terrific Greek sunset of the Aegean Sea one night, I wrote the following:

The Beauty

> I woke up this morning to the sound of a rooster crowing, a horse clopping down the alley, and a gentle breeze on the island of Hydra. To me, this is a scene of beauty that I have already locked away in my mind's eye. Athens provides an unusual study of beauty and contrast. I watch the Greeks confidently cross six lanes of traffic as cars zoom by. I hear the sounds of motorbikes and taxi cabs race off the starting line with a green light. Hearing the rumble of four million people moving 24 hours a day has been a new experience. These urban scenes carry a different kind of beauty from the sunset on the Aegean Sea, but there is a combined, complex beauty as these contrasting pieces come together.

During my Fulbright Specialist opportunity with Panteion University in Athens, I engaged in conversations at all university levels and connected with learners through workshops and conversations. I have learned much through this wonderful back and forth as I continue to develop new angles of leadership life stories. To me, there is a beauty in the opportunity to learn from these new friends and from seeing new possibilities open up in my writing.

In the Ugly

At this time, more than any other in my life, I hear people in and out of the classroom talk about panic attacks and anxiety. On another day, I wrote:

> Students are deeply worried in Greece and in the United States about whether classroom learning will translate to new jobs—if they can even get a job. Friends face shrinking salaries while executive leadership in companies are rewarded with six-figure salaries. Drastic cuts in organizations force individuals to find new jobs and some are even having to move to new industries to work and support family. Personally, I cleaned out my office before leaving because of the clear communication about a budget shortfall and people being permanently laid off.

Locally and globally, leadership seems to seek power instead of service, which puts families and communities on edge. Our townships, communities, provinces, states, and countries seem to be more divided than ever. This seems to cast an ugliness on what is happening every day. With all these pictures of ugliness, how do my Greek friends and John the Apostle help us find the beauty through leadership life stories? We know that, over time, John went from being a Son of Thunder to a caring personality by Mary's side at the cross. We know that he maintained a faithful witness, ministering to early church and writing even as he served out his last years in exile. John's life and his leadership life stories are direct witnesses to shalom with truth being learned over time.

Leadership Life Stories Principle:
A Posture of Learning

When John first meets Jesus, he still has a lot of learning to do. It is clear that he places himself in a posture of learning in several ways. We can learn from the posture that John adopts. Noticing what was important to John can help us as we develop our leadership life stories and as we continue to grow. Consider the following:

1. **As we learn, by grace, our growth is nurtured**. John is seen seeking and demanding, up to the moment he met Jesus. He loved God's truth early and he remained bold in proclaiming it to the very end of his life. There are not many gray areas in John's teaching—he is an either/or disciple. John started with a focus of making the grade and then discovered grace.

2. **Learning to love is central to our lifelong journey**. One might ask how John softened from a Son of Thunder to one known as the Apostle of Love, a humble brother who faithfully served the Lord for the rest of his life. The quality appears to be learned from Christ; spending time with a loving savior changes a person. It is interesting that John is characterized as a seeker of truth as he follows John the Baptist. We see a balance of truth and love in John, just as we do throughout Scripture.

Over the past few years, I have been honored to listen to and talk with individuals as they reflect on their leadership life stories. These times of joy and success and experiences of pain and struggle have influenced me as I think about and continue to develop the idea of leadership life stories and how they can be used in our personal and professional lives. For example, I reflect on the stories of student colleagues whose families immigrated to the United States with the hope of a better life only to be rejected by their new communities because they are different. Several of these young people are the first in their family to attend college or university. I think about the stories of friends who continue to take steps into organizational leadership positions, and I remember one who was asked to step down. I reflect on the stories of parents with struggling kids who balance the needs at work and the needs at home. I think about the student-athletes that I interact with each semester. One hockey player specifically realized that because of concussions, he would never play again. This young man is now trying to figure out the rest of his life. As I learn and grow through their stories, I vow to expand my knowledge so that I can share leadership life stories with more people.

Leadership Life Stories Principle: Persistence

In all these leadership life stories from the people in my life and from the leadership life story of John, I see a common value of persistence over time. Persistence is a whole-body activity with thinking and behavior that is aimed toward a goal. Some say persistence is continued action in the presence of obstacles. The finish line may be a few weeks or even decades down the road, so persistence is required. I like the quote that is commonly attributed to Benjamin Franklin that says, "Energy and persistence conquer all things." Where do your leadership life stories display persistence? I would like to suggest three areas for focus.

1. **Focus on motivation**. There are plenty of articles about internal (intrinsic) and external (extrinsic) motivation to review. This is commonly referred to as "finding your why" and can be seen in books like *The Purpose Driven Life*.[5] My motivation is a combination of internal and external factors that stem from my faith perspective. My hope is to make a difference in the lives of people I connect with each day so that they see the value of a personal relationship with Jesus Christ. What is the motivation that fuels your persistence each day?

2. **Focus on a goal**. Many of the college-level athletes I interact with are terrific examples of persistence as they focus intently on a goal. It takes persistence to train in the off season for something that is

months down the road. Remember that goals can be a double-edged sword. I appreciate the writing of Tom Holland, an athletic trainer who helps athletes finish triathlons. He offers three types of goals: (1) *outcome goals*, which essentially compare yourself with others; (2) *performance goals*, which compare yourself against previous performances; and (3) *process goals*, which "focus on improving a skill associated with your technique."[6] I use a combination of all three to maintain persistence in this area.

3. **Focus on an activity**. Persistence is about taking steps every day. There are times that getting up and starting something is the greatest barrier to overcome. For example, as we moved into the holiday season, the official start of training began for a run that I hope to complete in six months. As most of the United States is locked in below-average temperatures, we have added snow and ice to the challenge where I live. Yesterday I completed the recommended four-mile training run in blowing snow and a temperature of 12 degrees. My family thinks I am crazy. I had an absolute blast and preferred to think that this activity shows persistence.

Witnesses to Shalom: Cumulative Growth in Christ

I compare the step-by-step learning about leadership life stories much like our continued growth in our personal relationship with Jesus Christ. Growth does not take place overnight; it is cumulative. It requires patience and persistence. We must daily look to the Savior for strength and listen to his Word in Scripture. A posture of learning is required, for we can only accumulate growth if we learn from the day behind us. A good dose of humility is rolled into that posture of learning, for we cannot learn from others if we think we already know it all. When we focus on intentional steps of growth each day as John did, we may be blessed, too, with a lifelong legacy of learning and love.

Action Steps

John is called the beloved apostle, but his leadership life story was developed through the transforming work of Jesus Christ over time and through persistence. As you continue to develop your leadership life stories, consider the following questions:

1. **Step One**. What goal are you seeking to complete or to continue as you consider persistence?

2. **Step Two**. What are the first steps that you will take today to begin your focus on persistence?

As we move into the final chapter, please reflect on the progress you have made in your understanding of leadership life stories up to this point. What a joy to engage the good and challenging experiences of life and reclaim them for the joy found in Christ! Our final disciple, Peter, shows us how to make the journey of leadership life stories a part of our daily lives through the simple act of breathing in and breathing out.

Discussion Questions

1. Which of the three types of motivation do you prefer and why?

2. Can you think of a person—personal, local, or national—you see as someone who continues to learn and grow each day in their lives? How does this inspire you?

3. How has your leadership changed over time? What are some of the situations that have impacted this change?

Chapter 13

Peter: Leadership Life Stories
Built on the Rock

Humble yourself, therefore, under God's mighty hand, that he
may lift you up in due time.

—1 Peter 5:8

PETER IS DESCRIBED BY SOME AS the "duh-sciple" because, like many of us,
he is often hardheaded. Peter needed to be reminded often of his value. He
needed to be reassured that he was loved and treasured by Jesus. Peter is
one of the favorite disciples for most of us because of his big heart—a heart
that got him into big trouble several times. Most of us associate Peter with
his famous denials of Christ, but we may not recall that Jesus, after rising
from the dead, asked Peter three times to feed his sheep. Peter is truly a
witness to shalom. His leadership life stories reveal how Jesus can use our
greatest strength and our greatest weakness. Leadership life stories occur
daily as we breathe in and breathe out the strength of Jesus to point back to
our personal relationship with him.

Calling the Disciples: Peter

Peter is one of the disciples closest to Jesus. Peter is mentioned almost 200
times in the Gospels, and he plays an important role in the first-century
church.[1] Just like his brother, Andrew, Peter is a fisherman who is called to
ministry by Jesus. Peter, Andrew, James, and John were all fisherman and
were on the shores of the Sea of Galilee when Jesus walked by. The story of
Peter's calling is recorded in two of the Gospels (Matt. 4:18–22 and Luke
5:1–11). There is an added piece of his calling in John 1:41–42 that I want
to start with because this sets the tone for his witness to shalom.

In the Gospel of John, we read that Andrew went to find his brother
Simon after finding the Messiah and Andrew brought Simon to Jesus (John
1:41). This interaction between Jesus and Simon provides an important
starting point for the personality of Simon. Jesus acknowledges his name

(Simon) but immediately changes his name to Cephas, which means Peter. Both Cephas (Aramaic) and Peter (Greek) mean rock.[2]

I appreciate the back and forth with Peter and Jesus that we see later in the Gospel of Luke. It shows us the personality of Peter right from the start—he was hard-headed. Apparently because of the number of people following Jesus, he asks the fisherman to row out a bit so that he could be seen by all as he teaches. After completing the lesson (Luke 5:3), Jesus tells Peter to go to deep water "and let down the nets for a catch" (Luke 5:4). I can see the disbelief on Peter's face and hear it in his voice as he responds, "Master, we've worked hard all night and haven't caught anything. But because you say so, I will let down the nets" (Luke 5:5). I can hear the passive-aggressive tone in Peter's reply as he throws the nets over the side.

After the miraculous catch of fish and the boats almost sinking, Peter falls to the ground on shore and proclaims that he is a sinful man. I love this moment from Jesus as he directly calls Peter to ministry. Jesus says to Peter, "Don't be afraid; from now on you will fish for people" (Luke 5:10). Peter becomes the rock on which the early church is established and stands as a cornerstone even today. In some ways, Peter lives out his name physically, that is, hard-headed as he charges through life.

The Leadership Story:
Elements of Peter's Leadership

Peter's life exemplifies several important elements of a great leader; namely, the right raw material, the right life experiences, and the right character. Once he was called by Jesus, Peter took advantage of these elements and used them to the best of his ability for God's glory. Below, I have called them the "rights"—that is, the *right* raw material, the *right* life experiences, and the *right* character (which may make it sound as if Peter succeeded only because he was gifted with these qualities).[3] It is important to realize, however, that these could also be called the right responses. Peter's responses to life were governed by his love for Christ and by the Holy Spirit; he took what happened to him and used it, as a witness to shalom.

The Right Raw Material: Rock

Peter begins his life as a fisherman and later is called the "rock" of the early church. In the Gospel of John, we learn that Simon is his original name. Jesus tells him he "will be called Cephas" (John 1:42), which, we know, translates to "rock" in Aramaic.[4] When we think back on Peter's life, however, we remember him as a roller coaster of emotion and action. A firm, stable, and unmovable rock does not seem to be an appropriate symbol for the characteristics he often exhibits! Peter's emotions and actions often get him into trouble. In Matthew 14:22–33, fueled by his passion for Jesus, Peter steps out of the boat and tries to walk on water toward Jesus until he begins to sink. In Matthew 17:5, during the transfiguration of Jesus, Peter rushes around trying to build three shelters until God's voice from heaven interrupts and emphasizes that Jesus is the Christ. Peter's physical actions also got him into trouble. In Matthew 26:36–46, as Jesus is arrested in the Garden of Gethsemane, Peter draws a sword and cuts off the ear of Malchus. After the resurrection and the report of the empty tomb, Peter and John sprint to the site and Peter impulsively rushes in to see the folded burial clothes of the risen Christ (John 20:3 and Luke 24:12).

Peter speaks so effectively to us as a witness to shalom because we see his imperfections in our mirror. Most of us can relate to his emotions and behavior. This first-century leader had the same attitudes and behaviors that we still see today because of his humanity. Peter lived a life of strength and weakness, all under the umbrella of the saving grace of Jesus. Peter's life points not to Simon Peter, but to the grace of Jesus. Peter not only acknowledged his mistakes, but also accepted criticism.[5] If we can, in our humanity as Peter, live under God's grace, we too will point others to Jesus.

I'd like to offer a final thought on the right raw material. Peter is the first-century rock on which the twenty-first century church continues. In Matthew chapter 16, Jesus is having one of his teaching moments with the disciples. Jesus asks them, "Who do you say I am?" In verse 16 Peter has a wonderful moment of clarity when he replies, "You are the Messiah, the Son of the living God." I see Peter as truly understanding this moment in a flash of recognition. Scripture says that Jesus replies, "Blessed are you Simon son of Jonah, for this was not revealed to you by flesh and blood, but by my father in heaven" (v. 17). Everything points back to the firm, unwavering truth that Jesus is the Messiah. Our leadership life stories stand on that solid rock of Jesus. And just like Peter, the original rock of the disciples, our leadership continues in the world today.

The Right Life Experiences: Cross and Denial

Peter knew the feel of crushing defeat, and he also knew the greatest triumph found in Jesus. During the pivotal days of Jesus's crucifixion, Peter fell three times. In Matthew 26 we read that Jesus forecast that Peter would deny him three times. In a huff of self-righteousness, Peter tells Jesus he is wrong—only to immediately deny him three times. I think about Peter's final denial and the eye contact he may have had with Jesus in the moment the rooster crowed. What a crushing defeat for Peter!

Jesus, in his goodness, redeems this failure for his ultimate glory, and grace appears. In John 21:15–19, Jesus and Peter have an intimate back and forth moment. Jesus asks Peter three times to "feed my sheep" (v. 17). Peter understands that although he denied Jesus three times, Jesus forgives him for those three failings and entrusts him with the nurture and survival of his sheep, or those who follow him. In this communication exchange, I imagine Jesus and Peter, eyes locked, with Peter saying to the risen Savior, "Lord, you know that I love you." What a picture of amazing grace when Jesus replies, "Then, feed my sheep."

All of Peter's life experiences, even the difficult ones, were necessary to shape him into the man he needed to become by God's grace and love. Read the verse at the opening of this chapter again. In Peter's own words, you can hear the humility he learned. As a witness to shalom, he takes what he has learned and uses it to provide encouragement to the early believers.

The Right Character: Humility

Peter was not born humble. He learned humility through failure as he leaned on his Savior. I would suggest that it is only through failure that we learn and are able to take steps forward in our personal and professional lives. As a witness to shalom, Peter helps us learn that failure is an integral part of adult learning. Failure is when you put yourself out there, try something new, and do not succeed. This always results in initial disappointment, but when we lean upon the One who is greater, failure can also be a place where pivotal communication and our greatest leadership life stories are found. Failure can open new paths and new opportunities, but it works on our behalf only when we engage humility and rest in the strength of Jesus.

Leadership Life Stories Principle: Efcharisto

In and through leadership life stories, we can see that we are treasured more fully by Jesus than we can ever comprehend. It is not our good works that earn salvation. We are saved because of Jesus and his sacrifice on the cross, his defeat of death, and his resurrection from the dead. Out of this over-flow of love from Jesus, we are called to be disciples and serve as a witness to shalom every day. I believe we can do this by listening to and sharing leadership life stories.

I quickly fell in love with the sights, sounds, and tastes of Athens, Greece. When I arrived, I learned that there is a whole new level of using the language that is not translated through online videos. I tried to learn some of the language from those who spoke it before I left. One word I learned that is a cornerstone of my understanding of Greece is *efcharisto*, which means "thank you" in English.

I appreciate those who can break down individual words and go back to the Latin, Hebrew, or even Greek understanding of the root word for an added level of meaning. Trying out my Greek the first day I arrived, I came in after breakfast, armed with my American accent and a misplaced confidence of *efcharisto*. My attempt was to give thanks to our host. Instead, I received a lesson. Our host, Chrissio, explained that to her, *efcharisto* is an intentional breath in and a breath out of gratitude. Her research in early Greek and the meaning of the word connected its vocalization to its real meaning for me. The *ef-* sound that begins the word is the inhale, similar to moments that can take our breath away. Consider some examples. You may utter a quick inhale, the *ef-* of breath, at the delicious smell of coffee brewing in the morning; you might experience this catch of breath when overlooking Athens from the Acropolis or seeing a sunset just as it kisses the horizon or when hearing a statement from student and faculty colleagues at the University. All of these begin with gratitude and inhale. During lectures in Athens, Greece, I heard deep concerns about poverty, and I listened to the voices of those silenced. I listened to stories of panic attacks and tales of anxiety that so many felt. These moments of interaction were a quick inhale, the *ef-* of breath. These intake moments seemed like involuntary personal responses.

The *charisto* part of the word is the exhale, the settling into the emo-tion. This is where the brain and the body kick in after the initial moment. It can be signified by the groan that exhales after hearing disappointing news about the health of a family member, or it could be the satisfy-ing sigh after the first sip of coffee. The *-charisto*, the exhale, is involved rather than involuntary; it contains another sense or emotion; it signifies a whole-body involvement.

How does the inhale of *ef-* and the exhale of *-charisto* relate to the prac-tice of leadership life stories? Our leadership life stories surround us all day.

As our leadership life stories develop, we can share with others the inhale of *ef-* and the exhale of *-charisto*; we can experience the inhale of *ef-* and the exhale of *-charisto*, too, as they share their stories with us. As we communicate our stories to others and share their lessons, we show thankfulness for the successes and failures of life and for what God has shown us through these experiences. We can use the sharp intake of involuntary response to express the initial surprise or disappointment of an experience, followed by the exhale of whole-body involvement that moves us from shock to thanks.

Witnesses to Shalom

Just like the disciple Peter, we are all witnesses to shalom through the good and challenging moments of our leadership life stories. It is in these moments that we can realize the living, breathing peace and power of Christ working through our everyday lives. I appreciate Peter and his name "rock" not because he was unbreakable, but because he was willing to be shaped by the hands of Jesus. Are we, just like Peter, willing to be shaped by Jesus's hands?

Peter's leadership life story shows us that every failure and every success is not wasted. Each moment is threaded together through shalom which reflects back to the restoration and hope we have in Jesus Christ. In the quiet moments of leadership, the moments that nobody sees, we are a witness to shalom. When we forgive someone who has wronged us, when we take the time to mentor a struggling colleague, when we admit our own mistakes and learn from them, we are living echoes of Peter's witness.

At the beginning of the book, I highlighted that leadership life stories are different than just the regular life stories. Leadership life stories help individuals construct meaning out of their experiences in ways that inspire, guide, and influence both themselves and their communities and organizations. Unlike regular life stories, which can emphasize personal growth or overcoming tough times, leadership life stories are oriented outward, grounded in a process of shared meaning making. A leader takes the fragments of personal experience and, through faithful communication, interprets them in ways that offer insight, direction, and purpose to others.

Through leadership life stories we are breathing in the grace of God and exhaling his peace into a world that desperately needs it. Like Peter, we are invited to step boldly, stumble honestly, repent humbly, and keep telling the story of Jesus with our lives.

Leadership life stories are not always grand speeches or spotless resumes. They are the inhale and exhale of daily faithfulness, the surprise at God's mercy and the gratitude that flows back to him. Peter reminds us that our lives, when surrendered to Christ, become ongoing witnesses to shalom. Each of us, with all our imperfections and passions, have opportunities to be a witness today.

Action Steps

Peter wrote the book of 1 Peter for both the Jews and the Greeks. It is a testament to people of faith living in an unjust and broken world. It speaks to everyone who seeks a personal relationship with Jesus Christ. Peter continually points back to the overarching Glory Story and a personal relationship with Jesus as the cornerstone of our salvation. As we conclude this chapter and the process of leadership life stories, join me in reflecting on the moments of leadership that take your breath away in gratitude.

1. **Step One**. Set aside a few minutes today to think about the moments that provide an opportunity to *ef-* (inhale) and *-charisto* (exhale).

2. **Step Two**. Make a list of what you discover. Share those with someone. Do you know a leader who is discouraged? Maybe she can be encouraged by hearing about your ups and downs, but ultimately, your blessings in leadership. I would also love for you to share what you have discovered with me. Ultimately, thank God for those moments.

We live in a broken world that has small glimpses of the perfect shalom found in Jesus. We can engage these as agents of shalom and through models of shalom, and we can also use leaders who have gone before us as witnesses to shalom as examples. Jesus responded to Peter's declaration that Jesus is the Christ, the son of the Living God, by claiming that as a foundation as sure as rock. When we proclaim Jesus Christ as the foundation of our lives through our life leadership stories, we become rock-solid vessels through which shalom can flow.

Conclusion

We've come to the end of our journey. Now it is time to continue the steps learned with our families, our communities, and our organizations.

Throughout this journey, I have asked you to spend time in solitude, writing out your thoughts. I also asked you to share your stories with a close group of friends in your life. The final step here is to engage in our communities and organizations. I would like you to be open to the times that may present themselves for you to listen to or share a quick leadership life story. In these opportunities, try out the stories that you have now developed.

We began this book with a quote from leadership guru Warren Bennis that leadership "should always have room for inspirational stories about wonderful leaders as well as grim cautionary tales about bad ones."[6] Now is the time to begin developing our self-awareness about our leadership life stories so that we can be a witness through the seemingly simple act of storytelling in a broken world. The birth, death, and resurrection of Jesus to save humanity and offer the free gift of salvation to everyone is the overarching Glory Story that surrounds each of our individual leadership life stories. You have an opportunity to be a disciple of Jesus Christ by sharing your leadership life stories and engaging others to develop their stories under the grace and peace of Jesus.

At the beginning of this book, we discussed William Brassey Hole's painting. We saw 12 disciples in the boat, with Jesus walking on the water toward them. The chaos of our broken world engulfs us at times, but Jesus invites you to step into the chaos of a broken world and, with his help, to share a bit of shalom with those who are hurting. My life verse, Colossians 2:6–8, is a daily reminder from Scripture to live in Christ, being rooted and built up in him. I believe that we are strengthened in faith and overflowing with thankfulness when we listen to and share leadership life stories. Please reach out to continue the conversation. I'm looking forward to seeing where your leadership life story journey goes and how these leadership life stories provide shalom to our broken world.

Discussion Questions

1. How can sharing what you are thankful for in your journal benefit a leader who may be discouraged?

2. Do you feel that people are born leaders or are they forged in a fire? Which do you think is ultimately the strongest kind of leader and why?

3. Take a moment of vulnerability and share who or what your rock is. How is this acted on and displayed each day?

Notes

Introduction

[1] Boas Shamir and Galit Eilam, "What's Your Story? A Life-stories Approach to Authentic Leadership Development," *The Leadership Quarterly* 16, no. 3 (2005): 402.

[2] Annick Janson, "Extracting Leadership Knowledge from Formative Experiences," *Leadership* 4, no. 1 (February 2008): 73–94.

[3] Quentin J. Schultze, *Communicating for Life: Christian Stewardship in Community and Media* (Grand Rapids, MI: Baker Academic, 2000), 26.

[4] Lisa Sharon Harper, *The Very Good Gospel: How Everything Wrong Can Be Made Right* (New York: Waterbrook Press, 2016), 205.

[5] Walter Brueggemann, *Living Toward a Vision: Biblical Reflections on Shalom* (Philadelphia: United Church Press, 1982), 31.

[6] Cornelius Plantinga, Jr., "Educating for Shalom," Calvin University, March 19, 2024, https://www.calvin.edu/about/who-we-are/our-calling.html.

[7] Brueggemann, *Living Toward a Vision*, 66.

Chapter 1
Mapping the Journey

[1] Quentin J. Schultze, *Communicating for Life: Christian Stewardship in Community and Media* (Grand Rapids, MI: Baker Academic, 2000), 26–28.

[2] Walter Brueggemann, *Living Toward a Vision: Biblical Reflections on Shalom* (Philadelphia: United Church Press, 1982), 16.

[3] Annette Simmons, *The Story Factor: Inspiration, Influence, and Persuasion Through the Art of Storytelling* (New York: Basic Books, 2006), 183.

[4] Bernard M. Bass, *Bass & Stogdill's Handbook of Leadership: Theory, Research, & Managerial Applications* (New York: The Free Press, 1990), 11.

[5] Wilfred H. Drath and Charles J. Palus, *Making Common Sense: Leadership as Meaning-Making in a Community of Practice* (Greensboro, NC: Center for Creative Leadership, 1994), 3.

[6] Fred O. Walumbwa, Bruce J. Avolio, William L Gardner, and Tara Wernsing, "Authentic Leadership: Development of a Theory-Based Measure," *Journal of Management* 34, no. 1 (February 2008): 89–126.

[7] Robert Greenleaf, *Servant Leadership: A Journey into the Nature of Legitimate Greatness* (New York: Paulist Press, 1977).

[8] Don McAdams, *Stories We Live By: Personal Meaning and the Making of the Self* (New York: Guilford Press, 1997), 11.

[9] John MacArthur, *Twelve Ordinary Men* (Nashville, TN: Thomas Nelson, 2006), 174.

Chapter 2
James the Less: Life Stories Rooted in Christ

[1] National Park Service, Mammoth Cave National Park, Kentucky, USA, July 8, 2024. https://www.nps.gov/maca/learn/historyculture/african-american-history.htm.

[2] Kenan Christiansen, "In Kentucky, A Family at the Center of the Earth," *New York Times*, February 28, 2014.

[3] W. Brian Shelton, *Quest for the Historical Apostles: Tracing their Lives and Legacies* (Grand Rapids, MI: Baker Academic, 2018), 19.

[4] John MacArthur, *Twelve Ordinary Men* (Nashville, TN: Thomas Nelson, 2002), 171.

[5] Kristina Glicksman, *Salt and Light Media*, March 15, 2024, https://slmedia.org/blog/telling-them-apart-which-st-james-the-apostle.html.

[6] Asbury Smith, *The Twelve Christ Chose* (New York: Harper & Brothers, 1958).

[7] Walter Brueggemann, *Living Toward a Vision: Biblical Reflections on Shalom* (Philadelphia: United Church Press, 1982), 166.

Chapter 3
Thaddeus: The Elements of Formative Moments

[1] Asbury Smith, *The Twelve Christ Chose* (New York: Harper & Brothers, 1958), 139; W. Brian Shelton, *Quest for the Historical Apostles: Tracing their Lives and Legacies* (Grand Rapids, MI: Baker Academic, 2018), 211.

[2] Personal conversation, Einar Svansson, 2017; Google Translate.

[3] "Magnolia Plantation," March 15, 2024, https://magnoliaplantation.com/welcome.

[4] "Magnolia Plantation," March 14, 2024, https://magnoliaplantation.com/history.

[5] Annette Simmons, *The Story Factor: Inspiration, Influence, and Persuasion Through the Art of Storytelling* (New York: Basic Books, 2006), 183.

Chapter 4
Simon the Zealot: Commitment and Participation

[1] Tony Manfred, "18 Examples of Kobe Bryant's Insane Work Ethic," *Business Insider*, December 8, 2013, https://www.businessinsider.com/kobe-bryant-work-ethic-2013-12.

[2] Asbury Smith, *The Twelve Christ Chose* (New York: Harper & Brothers, 1958), 123.

[3] John MacArthur, *Twelve Ordinary Men* (Nashville, TN: Thomas Nelson, 2006), 175.

[4] Smith, *The Twelve Christ Chose*, 125.

[5] MacArthur, *Twelve Ordinary Men*, 177.

[6] Robert Greenleaf, *Servant Leadership: A Journey into the Nature of Legitimate Greatness* (New York: Paulist Press, 1977).

[7] Frank Dance, "Toward a Theory of Human Communication," in *Human Communication Theory: Original Essays,* ed. Frank Dance (New York: Holt, Rinehard, and Winston, 1967), 296.

[8] Walter Fisher, *Human Communication as Narration: Toward a Philosophy or Reason, Value, and Action* (Columbia, SC: University of South Carolina Press, 1989), Afterword, xii.

9 Wilfred H. Drath and Charles J. Palus, *Making Common Sense: Leadership as Meaning-Making in a Community of Practice* (Greensboro, NC: Center for Creative Leadership, 1994), 3.

10 T. S. Eliot, *Four Quartets* (New York: Harcourt Brace, 1943), 31 [italics in original].

11 Smith, *The Twelve Christ Chose*, 126–127.

Chapter 5
Judas Iscariot: Broken Leadership Life Stories

1 John MacArthur, *Twelve Ordinary Men* (Nashville, TN: Thomas Nelson, 2006), 176.

2 Asbury Smith, *The Twelve Christ Chose* (New York: Harper & Brothers, 1958), 144.

3 Glenn Schroder and Carol Wimber, *Never Trust a Leader Without a Limp: The Wit and Wisdom of John Wimber* (Nashville, TN: Thomas Nelson, 2020).

4 Anne Soetens, *Rotterdam Style*, March 23, 2024, https://rotterdamstyle.com/facts-stats/a-history-of-rotterdam-from-fishing-village-to-metropolis.

5 Anne Soetens, Rotterdam Style, March 23, 2024, https://rotterdamstyle.com/fact-stats._

6 A. B. Bruce, *The Training of the Twelve: How Jesus Christ Found and Taught the 12 Apostles* ([n.p.]: Pantianos Classics, 2018), 5707.

Chapter 6
Nathanael: Leadership Life Stories of Self-awareness

1 Walter Brueggemann, *Living Toward a Vision: Biblical Reflections on Shalom* (Philadelphia: United Church Press, 1982), 65.

2 A. B. Bruce, *The Training of the Twelve: How Jesus Christ Found and Taught the 12 Apostles* ([n.p.]: Pantianos Classics, 2018), 264; Shelton, *Quest for the Historical Apostles*, 159.

3 Bruce, *The Training of the Twelve*, 279.

4 Asbury Smith, *The Twelve Christ Chose* (New York: Harper & Brothers, 1958), 76.

5 Daniel Taylor, *The Healing Power of Stories* (New York: Doubleday Religious Group, 1996), 15.

6 Stephen Denning, *The Springboard Story: How Storytelling Ignites Action in Knowledge-era Organizations* (Boston: Butterworth-Heinemann Publishing, 2000).

Chapter 7
Thomas: Leadership Life Stories of Struggle

1 Asbury Smith, *The Twelve Christ Chose* (New York: Harper & Brothers, 1958), 98.

2 A. B. Bruce, *The Training of the Twelve: How Jesus Christ Found and Taught the 12 Apostles* ([n.p.]: Pantianos Classics, 2018), Kindle, 7853.

Chapter 8
Philip: Leadership Life Stories of New Perspective

[1] John MacArthur, *Twelve Ordinary Men* (Nashville, TN: Thomas Nelson, 2006), 126.
[2] W. Brian Shelton, *Quest for the Historical Apostles: Tracing their Lives and Legacies* (Grand Rapids, MI: Baker Academic, 2018), 145.
[3] Asbury Smith, *The Twelve Christ Chose* (New York: Harper & Brothers, 1958), 63.
[4] Smith, *The Twelve Christ Chose*, 66.

Chapter 9
Matthew: Leadership Life Stories of New Beginnings

[1] W. Brian Shelton, *Quest for the Historical Apostles: Tracing their Lives and Legacies* (Grand Rapids, MI: Baker Academic, 2018), 188.
[2] Asbury Smith, *The Twelve Christ Chose* (New York: Harper & Brothers, 1958), 82.
[3] Smith, *Twelve Christ Chose*, 81.
[4] A. B. Bruce, *The Training of the Twelve: How Jesus Christ Found and Taught the 12 Apostles* ([n.p.]: Pantianos Classics, 2018), 490.

Chapter 10
James the Greater: Son of Thunder

[1] John MacArthur, *Twelve Ordinary Men* (Nashville, TN: Thomas Nelson, 2006), 79.
[2] MacArthur, *Twelve Ordinary Men*, 88.
[3] Sigurgeir Jonsson, "The Volcanic Eruption of 1973," July 9, 2024, https://visit-westmanisland.com/volcanic-eruption-1973.
[4] Jeffrey Carlson, George Bassett, William Buehring, Michael Collins, Steven Folga, Brian Haffenden, Frank Petit, Jon Phillips, David Verner, and Robert Whitfield, "Resilience: Theory and Application," U.S. Department of Energy, Office of Scientific and Technical Information, January 2012, https://publications.anl.gov/anl-pubs/2012/02/72218.pdf.

Chapter 11
Andrew: Listening for Truth

[1] Asbury Smith, *The Twelve Christ Chose* (New York: Harper & Brothers, 1958), 29.
[2] W. Brian Shelton, *Quest for the Historical Apostles: Tracing their Lives and Legacies* (Grand Rapids, MI: Baker Academic, 2018), 110.
[3] Shelton, *Quest for the Historical Apostles*, 95
[4] Max DePree, *Leadership Is an Art* (New York: Bantam Doubleday Dell, 2008), 12.

Chapter 12
John: Cultivated through Time

[1] Asbury Smith, *The Twelve Christ Chose* (New York: Harper & Brothers, 1958), 51.

[2] W. Brian Shelton, *Quest for the Historical Apostles: Tracing their Lives and Legacies* (Grand Rapids, MI: Baker Academic, 2018), 127.

[3] Smith, *The Twelve Christ Chose*, 50.

[4] A. B. Bruce, *The Training of the Twelve: How Jesus Christ Found and Taught the 12 Apostles* ([n.p.]: Pantianos Classics, 2018), Kindle, 3743.

[5] Rick Warren, *The Purpose Driven Life* (Grand Rapids, MI: Zondervan, 2002).

[6] Tom Holland, *The 12-Week Triathlete* (Beverly, MA: Fair Winds Press, 2011), 19.

Chapter 13
Peter: Leadership Life Stories Built on the Rock

[1] John MacArthur, *Twelve Ordinary Men* (Nashville, TN: Thomas Nelson, 2006),

[2] A. B. Bruce, *The Training of the Twelve: How Jesus Christ Found and Taught the 12 Apostles* ([n.p.]: Pantianos Classics, 2018), 255.

[3] MacArthur, *Twelve Ordinary Men*, 39–48.

[4] W. Brian Shelton, *Quest for the Historical Apostles: Tracing their Lives and Legacies* (Grand Rapids, MI: Baker Academic, 2018), 61.

[5] Asbury Smith, *The Twelve Christ Chose* (New York: Harper & Brothers, 1958), 14.

[6] Warren Bennis, "Challenges of Leadership in the Modern World," *American Psychologist* 62, no. 1 (January 2007): 5.

Index

www.ingramcontent.com/pod-product-compliance
Lightning Source LLC
Chambersburg PA
CBHW020411130626
46549CB00006B/2522